AR IN THE ᵈDITERRANEAN AREA		WAR AT SEA		WAR IN THE AIR	
		OCT	*Royal Oak* sunk	SEPT	R.A.F. bombs German warships
		DEC	*Graf Spee* scuttled	NOV	German planes over Paris
NE	Italy invades France	JULY	Royal Navy cripples French Fleet	MAY	Rotterdam bombed
ᵛOV	Italy invades Greece	SEPT	British Fleet secures 50 U.S. destroyers for convoys	AUG OCT}	Battle of Britain
				DEC	Coventry bombed
ᶜEB	Germans land in North Africa	MAR	Royal Navy defeats Italian Navy	MAR	Heavy R.A.F. raids on Ruhr
ᴾL	Germans invade Yugoslavia and Greece	MAY	*Bismarck* sunk	JULY	Moscow bombed
ᴵNE	Germans capture Tobruk	APL	H.M.S. *Hermes* sunk	MAY	First 1,000-bomber raid on Cologne
ᶜT	Battle of El Alamein	AUG	H.M.S. *Eagle* sunk	JULY	R.A.F. attacks Ruhr in daylight
ᵛOV	Allied landings in North Africa	NOV	French Fleet scuttled at Toulon		
ᴬY	German and Italian surrender in North Africa	SEPT	Italian Fleet surrenders at Malta	MAY	R.A.F. destroys Moehne and Eder Dams
ᶜPT	Allied invasion of Italy	DEC	*Scharnhorst* sunk	AUG	U.S.A.F. bomb Ploesti Oilfields, Rumania
ᴱEC	Italy declares war on Germany				
ᴬR	Cassino destroyed	MAY	Normandy Invasion Fleet assembled	MAY	Railways and bridges destroyed in France
ᴶNE	Allies enter Rome	NOV	*Tirpitz* sunk	JUNE	Flying bomb
ᵁG	Allies invade Riviera				
ᴱEC	Civil War in Greece				
ᴬPL	Venice and Milan captured	APL	*Lü...*		...oyed

Armed Forces in Europe

D1081042

Duncan RA Macdonald
Mosers.

MODERN TIMES

Hitler and Germany

Titles in this series

Hitler and Germany

B. J. Elliott

WAVERLEY GRAMMAR SCHOOL, BIRMINGHAM

LONGMAN

LONGMAN GROUP LIMITED
Longman House, Burnt Mill, Harlow,
Essex CM20 2JE, England
and Associated Companies throughout the World.

First published 1966
Seventeenth impression 1984

ISBN 0 582 20425 9

Printed in Hong Kong by
Yu Luen Offset Printing Factory Ltd.

Acknowledgements

We are grateful to the following for permission to reproduce copyright material:

William Collins Sons & Co. Ltd for material from *Moscow Tram Stop* by H. Haape and D. Henshaw; The Hutchinson Publishing Group for material from *Mein Kampf* by Adolf Hitler, published by Hurst and Blackett Ltd; MacGibbon & Kee Ltd and Grove Press, Inc. for 'General, That Tank' by Bertolt Brecht, translated by Christopher Middleton, and '8th May, 1945' by F. B. Steiner, translated by Michael Hamburger from *Modern German Poetry 1910–1960: An Anthology with Verse Translations*, edited by Michael Hamburger and Christopher Middleton, Copyright © 1962 by Michael Hamburger and Christopher Middleton, and Odhams Books Ltd and Harper & Row, Publishers, Inc. for material from *Hitler—A Study in Tyranny* by Alan Bullock.

For permission to reproduce photographs we are grateful to the following: Anne Frank Stichting and Otto Frank—page 3; Associated Press—page 74; Barnaby's Picture Library—page 77; Fox Photos—pages 85 and 88; Giangiacomo Feltrinelli Editore—pages 11, 20, 62, 66, 71, 72, 80, 97, 142 and 156; Imperial War Museum—pages 103, 104, 132 and 136; Keystone Press—pages 36, 94 and 128; Österreichische Nationalbibliothek—page 89; Paul Popper—pages 8, 15, 28, 44, 68, 69, 106, 139 and 146; Radio Times Hulton Picture Library—page 16; Ullstein Bilderdienst—pages 6, 7, 18, 19, 21, 33, 46, 51, 54, 75, 91, 93, 110, 112, 119, 121, 134 and 145; Wiener Library—page 161.

The maps on pages 109, 116, 117, 123, 130 and 138 are based on some in Flower and Reeves, *The War 1939–1945*, by permission of Cassell and Company Limited, and those on pages 95 and 126 are redrawn from Bullock, *Hitler, A Study in Tyranny*, by permission of Odhams Books Limited.

Preface

Few people today under forty years of age have much personal recollection of Hitler's life. To a great many young people, he is simply a shadowy figure whose name is identified with terrible evils. I hope this book will shed some light on this shadowy figure.

I would like to acknowledge a deep debt to the immense labours of many distinguished historians, in particular Alan Bullock, William Shirer, Hugh Trevor-Roper and the late Koppel Pinson. Their work has done much to increase our knowledge and understanding of this fateful period of German history.

B. J. Elliott

Contents

Time Chart

This is a list of the main events in the life of Hitler and the history of Nazi Germany. It is recommended that they be studied carefully before starting to read this book. It will also help examination candidates if they can learn those dates marked with an asterisk.

1889	Birth of Adolf Hitler.
1908–13	Hitler in Vienna.
*1914–18	World War I.
*1919	Treaty of Versailles signed.
1920	Foundation of the Nazi Party.
*1923	Beer-Hall Putsch by Hitler.
1924	Hitler in prison—*Mein Kampf*, Vol. 1.
*1929	Beginning of the Great Depression.
1932	Nazis win 230 seats in elections.
*1933 Jan. 30	Hitler appointed Chancellor.
1933	Enabling law gives Hitler immense power.
1933	Trade Unions and political parties banned.
1934	Hitler murders his political opponents.
*1936	Occupation of Rhineland by Nazis.
*1938	Seizure of Austria by Nazis.
*1938	Munich Agreement.
*1939	Seizure of Czechoslovakia by Nazis.
*1939	German attack on Poland: World War II.
*1940	German invasion of Western Europe.
*1940	Battle of Britain.
1941	German invasion of Balkans and Russia.
1941	Japanese attack on Pearl Harbour: Germany declares war on U.S.A.
1942	Battle of El Alamein.
*1943	German surrender at Stalingrad.
1943	Allied invasion of Sicily and Italy
1944	D-Day.
*1945	Conquest of Germany: Hitler commits suicide.
1945–6	Trial of major German war criminals at Nuremberg.

Introduction

Four against Hitler

The twin-engined Mosquito light bombers began their long dive. It was nearly 4 p.m. and they had already flown 500 miles from Scotland across the North Sea. Safely over the Skagerrak they had now almost reached the head of the sixty-mile long Fjord and their target—Oslo.

Far below them in a block of three buildings close to the Royal Palace hundreds of men were gathering. They were attending a rally and march-past in honour of their leader, Vidkun Quisling. Suddenly the air-raid sirens blared out and those still outside the building stared skywards, their eyes searching the horizons. Their search ended abruptly; from over a hill to the south-east four dark shapes came swooping down onto the city. Even as they approached other dark shapes began to fill the sky—FW.190 fighters attacking the invaders with cannon and machine-gun fire. But the counter-attack had come too late; although one Mosquito plunged into the cold waters of Oslo Fjord, the remaining three bore down upon their target. Screaming over the roof-tops at barely 100 feet they unleashed their bombs over the large building where the rally was to begin. As he climbed away high above the city Squadron Leader D. A. G. Parry, D.F.C., the flight commander, looked back and saw a great cloud of red dust and smoke rising from the battered building. He then turned westward and with his two remaining companions headed back to Scotland.

In another European city 600 miles to the south-west of Oslo two families were sitting down to Sunday dinner. They were in a third-floor room at the rear of a large house. The house stood by a canal on Prinsengracht, a street in Amsterdam. The mother of one of the families spoke to the younger daughter of the other family.

'Come along, Anne, have a few more vegetables.'

'No thank you, Mrs Van Daan, I have plenty of potatoes.'

'Vegetables are good for you, your mother says so too. Here have some more.'

Anne Frank

A conversation you might hear at a million Sunday dinner tables; but this was not a typical Sunday dinner for the group sitting round the table. These seven people were in hiding for fear of their lives. For two-and-a-half months they had been living in two rooms shut off from the world by a secret door. They would remain hidden for another two years until they were betrayed. The girl who disliked vegetables was Anne Frank. She was thirteen years old and, like the other six people in the room, was a Jew.

Several hours later a Russian sergeant scribbled on a piece of paper:

'House captured. Await further orders.'

Crouching amongst the rubble of his prize already littered with his own and enemy dead, the Sergeant Jacob Pavlov knew nothing of Anne Frank's house 1,700 miles away. But he did know an attempt would be made to recapture his house. For sixty-two days Pavlov and his men held the house in the face of one vicious attack after another. Pavlov's house was in Stalingrad.

Far out in the South Atlantic a slight mist had risen over a calm sea. As the mist increased it had become increasingly mixed with smoke from a raging fire. The fire was raging aboard a ship, the S.S. *Stephen Hopkins*, bound from Cape Town to Paramaribo in Dutch Guiana. For twenty minutes shells and machine-gun bullets had been crashing against the hull and superstructure. At last with the main boiler burst, the deckhouse ablaze and the radio shot away the Captain had given the order—'Abandon ship'.

The *Stephen Hopkins* was going down fighting. As soon as the first shell had struck, Lieutenant Kenneth M. Willett, U.S.N.R., commander of the Armed Guard, had leapt to man the four-inch gun. Almost immediately shrapnel had torn a gaping wound in his stomach. In spite of his condition Lt. Willett fired off most of his thirty-five shells at his attackers. When his ammunition store had been blown up he had staggered down to the main deck to help to launch the life-rafts.

Thus passed a few hours in the lives of four people; an English airman, a Dutch schoolgirl, a Russian soldier and an American sailor. It was the last week-end of September 1942. These four had never met and they never will for only the Englishman and the Russian are still alive. Although separated by hundreds of miles of land and sea these four people were united in a fight. They were fighting to destroy a hideous evil which had gripped Europe: the empire of Adolf Hitler.

From the Volga to the Atlantic and from the Arctic Circle to the Sahara the forces of this one man ruled supreme. Ten million soldiers from Germany, Italy and Eastern Europe had marched in triumph through Paris, Brussels, Copenhagen, Warsaw, Athens and Kiev. In the factories and upon the farms of Germany untold millions slaved and sweated to supply his armies. In the dark alleys of Amsterdam and Belgrade and a hundred other cities men and women disappeared for ever into the night and fog. On desolate plains of Poland a thousand victims daily gasped and screamed as a silent death wrapped round them.

Such was Europe, the birthplace of modern civilisation, in September 1942.

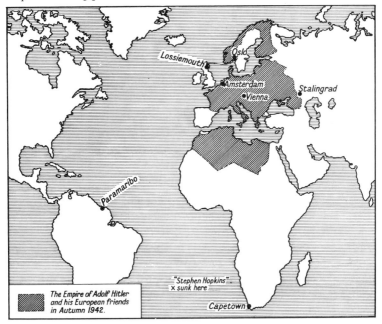

Four against Hitler

Squadron Leader Parry attacked that building in Oslo because it was the headquarters of the Gestapo, Hitler's monstrous secret police organisation. The men who were meeting there were traitors who had helped in the conquest of their own country, Norway.

Anne Frank hid in that room in Amsterdam because it was Jews who were being slaughtered every day in Poland. Anne was betrayed and died shortly before her sixteenth birthday, but her diary has survived. Sergeant Pavlov fought grimly in Stalingrad because it was in Russia that most of the German army was fighting in a savage bloodbath. Stalingrad had become the very centre of this cauldron and would cost a quarter of a million lives in less than half a year. Lieutenant Willett

5

German soldiers attacking in Stalingrad *Oi ! I cann see the pub from 'ere.*

died defending his ship against German merchant raiders because on Hitler's orders every Allied ship was to be sunk on
sight—ships which were the very lifelines of the Allied war
effort.

Four against Hitler. Who was this man Hitler? What forces
in his childhood, upbringing or adult life had fashioned such a
character? How had this man risen to be Lord of Germany?
How had he been able to trample underfoot a score of European nations and defy for a while the world's greatest powers?
To begin finding the answers to these and other related questions we must, from 1942, put the clock back thirty-three years
to 1909 and move to yet another great European city—
Vienna.

6

1 Hitler and the Coming of the Nazis: 1889–1933

The Emperor and the Tramp

Vienna in 1909 had a population of over two million people and was the capital city of the Austro-Hungarian Empire. It was a beautiful city standing on the banks of the blue Danube below the green hills of the Wienerwald. Less than fifty years had passed since its old medieval ramparts had been torn down and replaced by the vast and spacious Ringstrasse which encircles the city.

The Glory of Imperial Vienna—The Emperor's Sixtieth Anniversary

Tourists and residents alike stared in pride and wonder at the chain of magnificent buildings stretched along its length. The Parliament building of red, white and black marble; the City Church, the Hofburg Theatre, the Imperial Museum— all combined to create this 'shining circlet studded with semi-precious stones'. On a special day such as the Spring Parade, the Ringstrasse seemed a blaze of colour as lovely ladies and handsome officers jingled past. Princes and dukes, ambassadors and generals, all competed for the gasps of approval from the crowds lining the route. Finally there appeared the man who stood at the pinnacle of the Austro-Hungarian Empire's fifty million subjects—the seventy-nine-year-old Emperor, Francis Joseph—stiff, spare and eagle-eyed as his resplendent troops marched by. He had ruled Austria since 1848.

The Emperor Francis-Joseph, ruler of Austria for sixty-eight years

When the parade was over many sought rest and refreshment in the nearby Vienna Woods, the magnificent parks and woodlands which surrounded and penetrated into the city. By night the same crowds flocked to listen to the works of Europe's greatest composers—Beethoven, Mozart, Wagner and Vienna's own Johann Strauss. Directed by Gustav Mahler and later by Felix Weingartner, the opera in Vienna reached its greatest heights in the opening years of the twentieth century. In the superb Imperial Opera House, tended by 700 employees, the poor and wealthy alike could hear performances as fine as any in the world. In the space of a month performances as varied as *Lohengrin, Carmen, Tannhäuser, The Merry Widow* and *The Marriage of Figaro* could be heard. A lesser but still very popular attraction was the theatre, where the works of such writers as Alexandre Dumas, Henrik Ibsen and Oscar Wilde were performed. A three-week sensation in 1906 had been Buffalo Bill's Wild West Show, which included 500 horses.

Outside the places of entertainment under the bright light of arc lamps, electric tramcars rattled along. They were remarkably punctual and packed to the doors, having replaced the old horse-drawn trams seven years before.

As morning dawned again the casual stroller might see the children of Vienna pouring out of their homes and hurrying to one of the many dozen free public schools, lavishly built and equipped. Free books, pens, clothes, meals and even baths were provided when needed. Trips were arranged for the children to the hills by tramcar to escape the stifling heat of summer and medical care was available at one of the many hospitals built throughout the city.

On the surface Vienna in 1909 appeared to be a gay, prosperous, attractive and forward-looking city. But if an observant visitor had made a tour by night of the older and poorer areas instead of going to the opera, he would have found a very different picture. As the cold winter nights approached thousands of homeless men, women and children searched desperately for somewhere, anywhere, warm to sleep. For Vienna suffered from a chronic housing shortage. Nearly half the city's population lived in one- or two-roomed flats—in one block of flats 276 people lived in thirty-one rooms!

For those who could not afford even this cheap accommodation the alternatives were frightful. There were the Warming Rooms, where men sat on crowded benches at tables all night and women and children slept on the floor; where talking, smoking, coughing and snoring were forbidden. In illegal doss-houses people slept eighteen to a room and a late-comer might have to curl up on the window-sill. But the very depths of degradation were reserved for the sewer-dwellers—many on the run—who slept on beds of stone and straw and relied upon the foul-smelling gaseous air for warmth. For the fortunate few, however, there were the recognised 'Homes for Men'. It was at one of these in the Meidling District of the city that a tramp, Reinhold Hanisch, arrived on a cold October evening in 1909. He found an empty bed and then noticed a man next to him wearing nothing but an old pair of trousers. The man's clothes were being cleaned of lice, gathered from several days of sleeping rough. Hanisch inquired his name; the reply was, 'Adolf Hitler.'

So we have now found the future master and tyrant of Europe, penniless, jobless, louse-ridden, half-starved and homeless in a Vienna doss-house. He was then just twenty years old.

Hitler's Youth

Hitler was not a native of Vienna. He was born in the local pub at Braunau, a small village on the frontier with Germany. His father, a customs official, was a difficult and unstable man, who had been married three times. First to a woman fourteen years his senior, from whom he had become separated; within a month of her death he married a second time, but this wife soon died of tuberculosis. The third marriage, to Klara Pölzl, twenty-three years his junior, was the most successful, but of the five children born to them, only Adolf and his sister Paula survived infancy. Some of the father's stormy character obviously rubbed off on Adolf.

Father and son did not get on well, but Hitler was very fond of his mother—perhaps because she spoilt him a good deal. The ill-feeling which developed between Hitler and his father may well have been caused by unsatisfactory school reports.

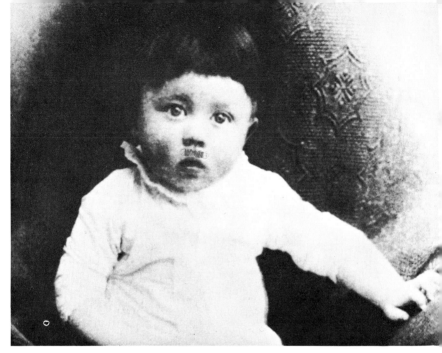

Adolf Hitler at the age of two years

Although he had done quite well at primary school, Hitler's performance at the Linz Realschule (technical school) brought continual criticism from his teachers. 'He lacked self-control and was proud, stubborn, bad-tempered and lazy,' said Professor Eduard Huemer in later years.

Hitler tried to excuse his poor school record by blaming his teachers. Also, many years later, he said: 'The majority were mentally deranged . . . absolute tyrants . . . their one object was to turn us into . . . educated apes like themselves.'

In his longwinded semi-autobiography *Mein Kampf* (My Struggle) Hitler claimed that the conflict with his father had grown from his refusal to follow in his father's footsteps as a customs official. 'I did not want to become a civil servant, no and again no. . . . One day it became clear to me that I would become a painter, an artist. . . .'

It was this ambition to become an artist which had led Adolf Hitler to Vienna. In October 1907 he had made application to enter the Academy of Fine Arts, but had failed. He returned to Linz five months later for his mother's funeral (his father had died in 1903), but then went back to Vienna.

So it was that, failing once more to gain entry to the Academy of Fine Arts, Hitler began a five-year period of aimless drifting. He lived in odd rooms and doss-houses, and worked casually as a snow-clearer, carpet beater and labourer. He did have some artistic talent and managed to sell some postcards and advertisement posters which he had painted. He dressed in threadbare second-hand clothes and often went hungry, unless he swallowed his pride and joined the soup queues. It was under these conditions that Hitler's ideas began to take shape. Vienna was Hitler's school.

The Mind and Ideas of Hitler

Vienna, as we have noted, was the capital city of the Austro-Hungarian Empire—a dying Empire. In 1909 it had only nine more years to live after a death struggle lasting well over half a century.

The Austro-Hungarian Empire was an artificial creation. It consisted of a dozen nationalities, including Poles, Czechs, Slovaks, Serbs and Croats. No natural frontiers or common language united them. A thousand years of victories and defeats in war, of treaties and marriages and hagglings had fashioned out the shape of this creaking dominion on the Danube.

Now it was breaking up. The Italians had already broken away and the Hungarians had secured equality (hence the name of the Empire). By 1909 the other subject races were noisily demanding equality and self-government. A general strike had secured the vote for all men in 1907, which meant that the German-Austrian ruling class could be outvoted. For the leaders of the Empire were German-speaking although not citizens of the German Empire. It was these German-Austrians who had once welded the Empire together and were now losing their grip on it.

To Adolf Hitler, who had become a fierce believer in German strength and unity while still at school, this was an unbearable situation. He thought the only way to hold the Empire together was for the German-Austrians to rule the subject races with an iron hand. Hitler's experience of the crumbling Austro-Hungarian Empire confirmed this belief in German supremacy. Throughout his life he became an ever more intense Nationalist. He believed that the German nation, which included all German-speaking peoples living on the fringes of Germany, was a master-race. As a master-race, they must become powerful, united and in possession of whatever land and materials they needed.

Hitler's love of the German people was soon balanced by hatred of the Jews. Most of you will know that eventually Hitler sent millions of Jews to their deaths. Anti-semitism (hatred of Jews) was not invented by Hitler. It had deep roots in Austria and in most parts of Europe. English kings had at times operated a 'protection racket' for wealthy Jews. Old wives' tales of Jewish rituals involving the sacrifice of Christian babies and other such horrors were forever circulating in medieval (and modern) Germany. In Poland and Russia periodic attacks on Jewish people and property were common in times of distress. Thousands of Jews fled to America to find freedom. It was easy to excuse such ill-feelings and violence by labelling the Jews 'Christ-killers'. The real cause of such feelings probably lay in jealousy, for throughout the ages the Jewish race has proved very skilful with money and in business dealings. Many of its members also reached the highest peaks of success in medicine, the law and in science—again providing a motive for jealousy.

Thus when Austria suffered from an economic depression in 1873 and many people were ruined or lost money, it was easy to blame the Jewish bankers such as the Rothschilds. A Viennese newspaper, *Deutsches Volksblatt* was full of anti-semitic stories and gossip. It told of a servant being beaten up by a Jew for smacking his seven-year-old boy after the boy had called her a 'dirty sow'. It reported that a Jewish cavalry officer had attacked his colonel with a drawn sabre at his court martial. (No such incident had in fact ever taken place.) It brought up the old fears of a Jewish 'take-over' of the universities by pointing out that while less than 9 per cent of Vienna was Jewish, 27·5 per cent of the students of the university were. Needless to say, it blamed the Jews for the organisation of vice rings, white slavery and drug peddling.

Hitler read the *Deutsches Volksblatt* and similar papers on many occasions, but at first he was not impressed. Then one day as he was strolling through the Inner City:

'I suddenly encountered an apparition in a black caftan and black sidelocks. Is this a Jew? was my first thought. For to be sure they had not looked like that in Linz. I observed the man furtively and cautiously, but the longer I stared at this foreign face, scrutinising feature for feature, the more my first question assumed a new form. Is this a German?'

To find an answer to this question Hitler buried his head into the vast anti-semitic literature available in Vienna. Soon the answer was clear. 'Was there any shady undertaking, any form of foulness, especially in cultural life, in which at least one Jew did not participate?'

We can find many reasons to explain why Adolf Hitler came to hate the Jews. They are an international race, while Hitler was a fervent Nationalist. There were many wealthy Jews in Vienna in 1909. Hitler was desperately poor and indeed often resorted to Jewish charities for help. Hitler was 'a shy and lonely man and must have watched blonde German girls walking in the company of what he later called 'repulsive, crooked-legged Jew bastards'. Perhaps most of all they provided a scapegoat, a reason for failures: personal failures, financial failures, military failures and political failures of which we shall hear more later. Hitler's belief in a 'master-race' explains why he was not attracted to socialism or communism.[1] Both proclaim the equality of men. Neither would he tolerate free speech and a free press nor rule by parliament, which gave, in theory, all men an equal say in government. The half-starved tramp who roamed the streets of Vienna needed this faith in himself as a member of the 'master-race'. Otherwise he would have been no better than the Czechs, Slavs and Jews whom he passed in the street. He had no sympathy for his fellow unfortunates in the slums of Vienna. 'It is not by the principles of humanity that man lives or is able to preserve himself but solely by means of the most brutal struggle.'

Life to Hitler had indeed become a brutal struggle against physical want (food, clothing and shelter). Later it would be against the governments and political parties of Germany. Finally he was to drag Germany into a fight to the death against the world's greatest powers. In such a struggle there were no rules. He would cheat and twist, bully and plead. He

[1] See glossary on page 167.

trusted no one, though others sometimes trusted him. No method was too low and underhand if it worked successfully. No lie was too big; the bigger it was, he believed, the more likely people would believe him. But the final argument, the final means of persuasion, was force. Ruthless and violent force: this was the key with which Hitler would unlock many doors, but which finally and fatally rebounded upon him.

Munich as Hitler would have known it in 1913

Corporal Hitler

In May 1913 Hitler left Vienna, and he did not return for twenty-five years. He went to live in Germany, in Munich, claiming that he could no longer bear the multi-racial atmosphere in Vienna. The real reason for his departure may have been to avoid being conscripted into the Austrian Army. Hitler denied this, claiming that he had been turned down as medically unfit.

15

Whatever the reason for his move, Hitler soon found lodgings, in Munich, with a tailor's family by the name of Popp. He made a desperate sort of living out of painting posters and postcards, and spent most of his spare time reading. He had already taken to spending much of his time in public libraries in Vienna, but his reading was unplanned and ranged over a wide variety of subjects. Eventually his reading became simply a means of confirming what he already believed. The ideas and opinions of Adolf Hitler were rapidly hardening into burning obsessions.

Hitler amongst the huge crowd in Munich which joyfully greeted the declaration of war in 1914

Some fifteen months after Hitler arrived in Munich, the First World War broke out. He saw it as Germany's fight for survival and welcomed it wholeheartedly. Now after six years of aimless drifting he saw his purpose in life, joining in this mighty struggle. He was happy and excited. 'I sank down upon my knees and thanked Heaven out of the fullness of my heart for the favour of having been permitted to live at such a time.' Early in August 1914 he joined the 16th Bavarian

Reserve Infantry Regiment, serving until 1920 and reaching the rank of corporal.

Germany, Europe and World War I

Hitler's departure from Austria in 1913 had taken him out of the crumbling Empire into one which was almost brand new. Only forty-two years had passed since the jigsaw collection of German states had become finally moulded into the German Empire under William I. During these forty-two years Germany's strength and power had increased enormously. In the production of coal, iron and steel, the sinews of war, she had quickly begun to challenge Britain and then passed her. Her army was the finest in the world, a million strong, and since the early 1900s she had been engaged in an enormously expensive battleship-building race with Britain.

Britain in 1913 had seen her position as the world's leading industrial power slipping, being overtaken first by the U.S.A. and then passed by Germany. Britain was still the world's greatest sea and trading power in spite of Germany's efforts, and her empire covered one-quarter of the globe. Germany's empire-building had begun too late (1880s) and she felt a certain jealousy towards Britain. France was also a great colonial power, mainly in north and west Africa and south-east Asia. A great defeat by Germany in 1871 and the threat of the Triple Alliance (Germany, Austria-Hungary and Italy) had led to France's alliance with Russia (1893). Russia was a doubtful ally. Unrest at home and the threat of revolution were shaking the throne of the Tsar (Emperor), Nicholas II. Her defeat on land and by sea at the hands of Japan (1904–5) had lowered her military reputation. France had already turned to her old enemy, Britain, and accepted the hand of friendship in the 'Entente Cordiale' (1904).

Thus Europe in 1913 had divided into two great armed camps ready for the war which most people believed was inevitable. The United States of America, already the world's leading industrial power, took no part in these proceedings. The wild West had barely been tamed and it was only in the previous year (1912) that the last two mainland states, Arizona and New Mexico, had joined the Union. Americans

The first recruits for the German Army in 1914

were understandably too busy making themselves and their country wealthy to be bothered about sabre-rattling in Germany and elsewhere. It was not until the third year of the War (1917) that America finally took sides and threw her crushing weight into the scales against Germany.

Adolf Hitler was in the thick of the fighting on the Western Front, the network of trenches stretching from the North Sea coast for 450 miles through Belgium and France to the Swiss frontier. He witnessed the horrible slaughter by machine-guns as hundreds of thousands of French, German, British and Colonial troops charged and recharged over the muddy, cratered ground. One bullet found its mark in his leg. He watched coughing, stumbling figures walking back from the front, blinded by mustard gas, each clutching the belt of the man in front. He was to follow them into hospital and was only recovering his sight when the war ended. He cheerfully ate the black bread and drank the artificial coffee to which Germany had been reduced by the Allied naval blockade. 'But', the propaganda leaflets and newspapers would tell him, 'Britain is near to starvation thanks to the gallant efforts of our

A German aid-post on the Western Front. Hitler was wounded twice

Fuck me! That were some party.

submarine crews, who are sinking every merchant vessel which approaches her shores.'

So Adolf Hitler cheerfully put up with the rain which filled the trenches knee-deep, sometimes even waist-deep. He managed to ignore the whistle of machine-gun bullets and the dull thump of shells, and to hurl himself face down into muddy shell holes when the firing grew too hot. For although not a front-line soldier he had a job almost equally dangerous, that of regimental runner, carrying messages from headquarters to the trenches and back. On one such mission it was later claimed, he captured single-handed several French soldiers, for which he was awarded the Iron Cross, First Class. There is no written record of this incident, however.

Men who served with him thought him rather 'peculiar'. Often he would leap up in the barracks and begin attacking the Communists and Jews. He received no letters or parcels and unlike other soldiers did not grumble or curse the war. He went home on leave to Munich only once and was shocked. Everywhere he seemed to see dodgers and shirkers, black-marketeers and war profiteers. From everybody's lips he heard

Queueing for the potato ration in Berlin, 1917

grumbles and complaints about the shortages and hardships brought about by the war. How, he wondered, could the armies at the front succeed when they were given such poor support at home? Soon he began to see this lack of support as a form of sabotage. The German army was being 'stabbed in the back'.

Germany in Defeat

One Sunday, 10 November 1918, when Adolf Hitler was in hospital recovering his sight, a padre brought him news which, for the first time since his mother's death, caused him to break into tears. That morning the Kaiser (Emperor of Germany) had given up his throne and fled to Holland. The day before, Germany had been declared a Republic and on the following day an armistice would be signed with the Allies. Germany was defeated. Hitler almost collapsed. He threw himself on his bunk and sobbed. 'So it had all been in vain. In vain all the sacrifices and privations . . . in vain the hours in which, with mortal fear clutching at our hearts we nevertheless did our duty; in vain the death of two millions. . . . Had they died for this? . . . So that a gang of wretched criminals could lay hands on the Fatherland?'

The 'wretched criminals' to whom Hitler referred were the democratic parties of the Reichstag (Parliament), mainly the Social Democrats. They had been thrust, somewhat unwillingly, into power by the collapse of the imperial-military regime (that is the government controlled by the Kaiser, his son Prince Max, and the army generals Lüdendorff and Hindenburg). During the last two years of the war this group had been in complete control of Germany's government and war effort. They had taken great care to see that no news had been released telling the people of defeats, retreats, hardships or shortages. Newspapers and bulletins had proclaimed a constant stream of advances and victories. The result of Germany's desperate military position in September 1918 had led Lüdendorff to demand an armistice. When news of this leaked out, which meant nothing more or less than an admission of defeat, most Germans were thunderstruck. Not until 2 October were the political party leaders told of the seriousness of the situation on the Western Front. Von Heydebrand, leader of the Conservative Party, ran up and down shouting, 'We have been deceived and cheated'.

REVOLUTION

General Lüdendorff had suggested that the Social Democrats should join the government in the hope that they would get

Men of the High Seas Fleet who sparked off the Revolution in 1918

better peace terms from the Allies. The Socialists had been opposed to Germany's wartime plans of seizing other nations' territories so it was hoped the Allies would treat them more kindly. In taking in the Social Democrats, Lüdendorff was merely anticipating events, for his rule was already failing fast.

It was German sailors at Kiel who lit the fuse of revolution. A rumour began to pass round the fleet that a suicidal charge was to be made against the British Grand Fleet, a much stronger force. To men on short rations and low pay, cooped up in harbour under stern discipline, this was the last straw. A mutiny broke out and demonstrators were fired upon.

The workers of Kiel seized this opportunity to set up a Workers' and Soldiers' Council to govern the town. This was based on similar bodies set up in Russia the previous year at the time of the Communist Revolution. Other cities such as Hamburg, Dresden, Cologne and Hanover followed suit. Meanwhile in Berlin the Socialist leaders were working hard to secure the armistice terms and the abdication of the Kaiser. Only the threat of a general strike in Berlin and the knowledge that the garrison would join them convinced the Reich Chancellor (Prime Minister), Prince Max of Baden, that he must yield. He handed over his office and powers to Friedrich Ebert, and at 2 p.m. on 9 November Philipp Scheidemann, leader of the Majority Socialists (the Socialists were split into two groups), stood on the Reichstag Balcony and proclaimed: 'Workers, soldiers, the German people have triumphed all along the line. . . . Long live the great German Republic.' One man who did not join the cheering was the half-blinded Adolf Hitler.

'I knew' [he said] 'that all was lost. Only fools, liars and criminals could hope for mercy from the enemy. In these nights hatred grew in me, hatred for those responsible for the deed. Miserable and degenerate criminals! . . . My own fate became known to me. I decided to go into politics.'

CIVIL WAR

Meanwhile in Berlin the revolutionary government led by Ebert was in a difficult position. On one side the Communists were pressing for nationalisation of industry and the abolition of the army; while the army itself, returning from the front, had hopes of destroying the revolution and assuming power. Accordingly Ebert was forced to make a bargain with General Groener that his government would smash the Communists and keep the army intact. In return the army would support the government. Already, therefore, the authority and power of the revolutionary government had been seriously weakened.

This secret agreement was soon put to the test. In December the Soviet leaders from all over Germany met in Berlin demanding the abolition of the army. This was followed by an attack on the Chancellery Building, and Ebert called upon the army for help. The rebels, called Spartakists, after Spartacus, the leader of a slave rebellion in ancient Rome, were in a strong position. Their leaders, Karl Liebknecht and Rosa Luxemburg, demanded that Germany should follow Russia's example in matters of government. But early in the New Year the army, assisted by irregular forces, struck and crushed the Spartakists after several days' savage fighting. The two leaders were shot. Rosa Luxemburg was brutally beaten up first, and finally her body was thrown into a canal. It was not recovered for five months.

Hitler had returned to Munich soon after the Armistice. Revolution had broken out here also when Kurt Eisner, a Jewish writer and member of the Social Democrat Party, had proclaimed a republic and assumed control of the government. In the New Year, at the time of the Spartakist revolt in Berlin, Eisner's party was heavily defeated in state elections. A month later Eisner was murdered by Count Anton Arco-Valley, a young student, and in the troubled months that followed Bavaria found itself with three rival governments. Soon after Eisner's death the Majority Socialists established themselves in Nuremberg. On 7 April 1919 the Independent Socialists set up a Soviet government in Munich. Two days later the Communists also proclaimed their own Soviet in Munich.

The Majority Socialists, like Ebert in Berlin, had to call upon the army and the Free Corps to sustain their authority. For nine days Munich became the scene of bloodshed and brutality. Civilians and hostages were murdered, prisoners were beaten and executed without trial. By the time the government troops had secured control 557 persons had died. The Social Democratic Government was in turn overthrown by the army and the Free Corps. A right-wing militarist government was set up which gave shelter to the extremist parties which were rapidly growing up.

Hitler was in Munich during these troubled times. In *Mein Kampf* he claimed to have escaped arrest by threatening his attackers with his rifle. After the rebellion had been crushed, he secured his first post in 'politics'. He became an 'instruction officer' with the task of lecturing the troops against the evils of Communism, pacifism and democracy. In September 1919 he was given a fateful order. He was sent to investigate a new political group which had been meeting in Munich for eighteen months. It was called the German Workers' Party. Hitler later renamed it the National Socialist German Workers' Party, but to the world it has become notorious by its abbreviation—the NAZI Party.

The Weimar Republic, 1919

In the midst of this violence and bloodshed, the Socialists carried out their promise of an early election. This took place in January of 1919. The Majority Socialists gained the largest number of seats, 165 out of 423, but as this was only 39 per cent they could govern only with the support of other political parties.

The new National Assembly met not in riot-torn Berlin, but in the sleepy town of Weimar, a cultural centre which has been compared to Stratford-on-Avon. From this town came the name of the Republic which was to rule Germany for the next fourteen years. The assembly found itself faced by three main tasks:

1 To create a lawful government to replace that put into power by the revolution.

2 To make peace with the Allies. (The Armistice was only a cease-fire.)

3 To draw up a new constitution for the Republic.

Friedrich Ebert was elected President by 73 per cent of the deputies (M.P.s), but to form a majority government the Socialists had to call on the support of the Centre and Democratic Parties. This need for a coalition government was one of the heavy burdens under which the Republic struggled throughout its short life. In addition many judges and civil servants were opposed to the Republic.

The table below shows the number of seats held by each party at various times during the Weimar Republic. You can see quite clearly that the Social Democrats never had a absolute majority which would allow them to rule with firmness and determination.

	1919	1924	1930
Nationalists	44	103	41
People's Party	19	51	30
Centre Party	91	69	68
Bavarian People's Party	—	16	19
Democratic Party	75	32	20
Social Democrats	165 }	131	143
Independent Social Democrats	22 }		
Communists	—	45	77
Nazis	—	14	107

(You can find out what each of the above parties stood for in the glossary on p. 167.)

THE TREATY OF VERSAILLES, 1919

It was hoped that the new form of government would be looked on with favour by the Allies and that the now humbled and repentant Germany would be received back into the world family of nations. These hopes were in vain.

THE MOOD OF THE ALLIES

When Germany asked for an armistice in 1918 the Allies were feeling very bitter. The French especially felt that Germany should be made to pay for the damage she had done, even though the million-and-a-half French dead could not be brought back to life. The British, having lost less, were not as bitter as the French, but many Conservative and Liberal M.P.s joined in the cry of 'Hang the Kaiser', and Lloyd George, the British Prime Minister, spoke of squeezing Germany until 'the pips squeaked'. General Pershing, the American commander, didn't want peace at all. This was because his troops were still fresh and he wanted to capture Berlin.

These feelings had not died down when the Allies met in Paris to discuss peace terms, so it came about that a document was drawn up designed to incriminate, punish and permanently weaken Germany.

THE TERMS OF THE TREATY

There were over 400 articles to the Treaty, the most important being as follows:

1 *Armed forces.* The German army was to be reduced to 100,000 men. Germany was not to be permitted to possess or build aeroplanes, submarines, large warships or tanks.

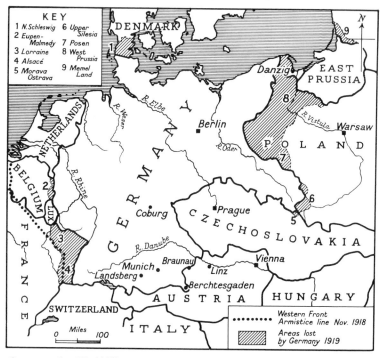

Germany after World War 1

2 *European territories* (see map above). Germany was to surrender Alsace-Lorraine to France and to give the coal from the rich Saar mines to France for fifteen years. Eupen-Malmédy was to be given to Belgium and North Schleswig to Denmark. In the east a huge slice of land (West Prussia and Posen and parts of Silesia) was given to Poland. This cut off East Prussia from the remainder of the German Republic.

3 *Overseas empire*. Germany had to surrender all her overseas territories in Africa, China and the Pacific. They were taken over by the Allies along with all German property in them.

4 *War guilt*. Germany and her Allies had to accept full responsibility for all damage and losses in the war. An enormous sum of money (later settled at £6,600 million) was to be paid to Belgium and France in compensation. As guarantee against further attacks, Germany had to remove all troops and military installations from the east bank of the Rhine. Allied troops were then to occupy bridgeheads along the river. France, outnumbered three to two by Germany, wanted the formation of an International Army to punish aggressors. When this was rejected by the Allies, it was decided to use the Rhine as a defensive 'wall'. Germany was therefore forbidden to place troops within thirty miles of the Rhine for the next thirty years.

5 *The League of Nations*. President Wilson of the U.S.A. insisted that a plan for the formation of a League of Nations should be included in the Treaty. The League had two purposes—to prevent war and to bring about international co-operation. Although some success was achieved by the International Labour Organisation (a branch of the League), and in dealing with the problems of slavery, refugees and drug-peddling, the League was a failure. Lacking the support of the U.S.A., Russia until 1934, and Germany after 1933, the League was unable to prevent fighting and squabbling in many parts of the world. The greatest failure of the League was the outbreak of World War II. The blame does not lie with the League, which had no army or police of its own. The member states were only too ready to put their own national interests before those of the League. If these interests led to war, the League had no actual power to stop it.

THE EFFECT UPON GERMANY

The National Assembly had known of the terms of the Treaty for several weeks before the actual signing was to take place. On 12 May 1919 the party leaders had, one after the other, rejected the terms.

'A terrible and murderous attack', declared Prime Minister Scheidemann. 'No, and a second time, No, and a third time

No!' said Professor Quidde, a pacifist. 'This peace we cannot accept', said Fehrenbach, the President of the Reichstag. These were brave but empty words. The National Assembly had no choice but to accept the dictated peace. The Allied navies had been maintaining the blockade of German ports since the Armistice. This had resulted in great suffering, even famine, during the winter of 1918–19. In Cologne, British

German delegates leaving the Palace after signing the Treaty of Versailles

occupation troops gave away their own food to starving German children. Refusal to sign the Treaty would have made the lives of most Germans unbearable through the maintenance of the blockade. Refusal would also have led to an Allied invasion of Germany. The exhausted German army was in no state to resist further attacks. Accordingly, the National Assembly agreed, by a vote of 237 to 138, to sign the Treaty.

On 28 June 1919 Hermann Muller of the Majority Socialists and Johannes Bell of the Centre Party travelled to France to sign on behalf of Germany. The actual signing took place in the famous Hall of Mirrors at the Palace of Versailles, near Paris. The choice gave revenge to France, for it was in this very room, less than fifty years before, that William I had been proclaimed the first Kaiser of the Second Reich. This had followed upon the defeat of France by Prussia (the largest kingdom in northern Germany).

The *Deutsche Zeitung* ('German News') spoke for a great many Germans when on the morning of the signing it carried the following front-page statement:

VENGEANCE! GERMAN NATION!

Today in the Hall of Mirrors of Versailles the disgraceful Treaty is being signed. Do not forget it! The German People will, with unceasing labour, press forward to re-conquer the place among the nations to which it is entitled. Then will come vengeance for the shame of 1919.

It was from such feelings that the 'stab-in-the-back' legend grew. Weimar politicians were accused of having stabbed the army in the back; the Socialists were accused of treachery, leading to Germany's surrender while the army remained un-defeated in the field. Those who had signed the Armistice of November 1918 were often called the 'November Criminals'. In a speech a few years later Hitler shouted that the only place for these men was the gallows.

THE WEAKNESS OF THE TREATY OF VERSAILLES

World War I was fought to prevent Germany from becoming the master of Europe. Some British politicians were not slow to point out that the Treaty came close to making France temporarily the master. Having prevented Germany from conquering Europe, the Allies were determined to end the German 'menace' for ever. The Treaty aimed at weakening Germany, but relied mainly upon the Germans to carry it out! The immense reparations payment had to be collected by the German government and handed over to the Allies. The dis-armament of her forces and the surrender of war materials was

2*

in the hands of her government. There was an Inter-Allied Commission of Control which sent inspection teams around the country, but they relied upon the co-operation of German officials. Thus during inspections the giant steel firm of Krupps was able to disguise long gun-barrels as chimneys! The Control Commission was powerless to prevent Krupps buying control of the Bofors armament firm in Sweden. In Holland and Spain submarines were built and crews trained for the German Navy. Following the Treaty of Rapallo in 1922 schools were set up in Russia for the training of German troops with the forbidden weapons—heavy artillery, tanks, aeroplanes and poison gas.

The territorial clauses of the Treaty of Versailles took away many of Germany's richest lands. Iron ore from Lorraine and coal from the Saar and upper Silesia were of the greatest importance to Germany's manufacturing industries: but to earn the money to pay the reparations, Germany needed to make and export goods. In addition, her main markets were overseas and the Treaty had all taken away the whole of Germany's merchant navy.

The greatest weakness of the Treaty was that it did not end the German 'menace' by means of the punishment clauses. The German Empire was left basically intact. Although Germany did lose some territories, by far the major part of her strength (land, population and resources) was untouched. Thus Germany, angered and embittered by the Treaty, had only to reject it at some future time and she would be almost as strong as she had been in 1914, if not stronger.

Though temporarily weakened Germany was still the greatest power on the continent. The collapse of Russia into revolution and civil war took away her main rival. In terms of population and industrial strength, France's strength did not amount to two-thirds that of Germany.

In 1919 most statesmen realised this, but hoped that Germany had learnt her lesson, that is, not to try to get what she wanted by war. For many years it seemed as if their hopes were justified.

Finally, the majority of Germans were determined to abandon the Treaty as soon as it was safe to do so. To be successful the Treaty had to be enforced, and in the last resort the only way to enforce it was by restarting the war. What man in the 1930s was willing to bring back the bloodbath of 1914–18 for the sake of a few square miles of central Europe?

By 1935 much of the bitterness of 1919 had evaporated. Many people in Britain and France had begun to feel guilty about the severity of the Treaty. When Hitler began rearming and making threatening gestures these feelings helped to prevent firm action by the Allies.

When Germany did finally renounce the Treaty and begin rearming in 1935, the Western Powers could only sit tight.

THE EFFECTS OF WORLD WAR I

The armistice of November 1918 did not, as we have seen, bring back peace and prosperity to Germany. For much of the world the years immediately after the war were also a period of trouble. Unemployment, political unrest and even civil war were the fate of many countries. In 1919 an epidemic of influenza swept around the world, killing about 20 million people.

Only the U.S.A. emerged stronger and richer. The Allies owed her £2,000 million and not until 1931 did America cancel these debts. Although her power had played an important part in the final victory, America soon turned her back on the world. She refused to sign the Treaty of Versailles, thereby remaining outside the League of Nations; and limited immigration from war-torn Europe.

France, with $1\frac{1}{2}$ million dead (one man per minute for the first two-and-a-half years), was obsessed by fear of Germany. This fear almost became a paralysis. The devastation of her coalfields and agriculture gave strength to her demand for war damages from Germany.

Britain, with 'only' three-quarters of a million dead had escaped more lightly. The enormous cost of the war, however, had turned Britain from being a creditor nation (selling more than she bought) to being a debtor. Instead of being the 'workshop of the world', Britain now found herself trying to sell her goods in the face of fierce foreign competition and rising tariff barriers. The loss of these overseas markets created unemployment and unrest in Britain. Britain's great sea power was now equalled by that of the U.S.A.

Russia was in ruins. Three years of war against Germany

and Austria had been followed by revolution, a bloody civil war and finally a terrible famine. During the ten years following the outbreak of World War I, the population of Russia was reduced by 20 million! In addition, as the world's first Communist country, Russia was regarded with intense distrust by most of the Great Powers. During the civil war some had actually sent troops into Russia to help the anti-Communist forces.

Japan had fought on the side of the Allies, but her leaders were not happy with the outcome. They felt that they were being treated as inferiors by the 'white' races. When their claim to Chinese territories was rejected and their navy was limited to three-fifths of that of the U.S.A. and Britain (1922), anger and resentment began to grow.

Another victor of World War I, Italy, was also dissatisfied with their share of the fruits of victory. Italy had entered the war against Germany following the secret Treaty of London, 1915. Britain and France had promised Italy lands across the Adriatic Sea and overseas colonies. These promises were never fulfilled. Following the usual pattern of the time Italy suffered from strikes, unemployment and unstable governments. To fight growing Communism, a journalist and former army sergeant, Benito Mussolini, formed a group called Fascists. They wore black shirts and used violence and terror to get what they wanted. Mussolini seized power in 1922 and won the admiration of Hitler. Later they were to become friends and allies, joined by Japan.

Eastern Europe suffered great changes following World War I. Austria became a weak, unsteady republic with a population of only 7 million. Two of the newly independent states, Finland and Hungary, were torn by civil war. Poland, reborn after over 100 years of foreign rule, took advantage of Russia's troubles to attack her and secure extra lands. Turkey, having lost her empire, became a republic and was soon engaged in a war with Greece.

Most Germans, however, believed that they had come off worst. Two million of her best young men were dead, the treasury was empty, and the country would be deeply in debt for many years ahead. The Treaty of Versailles had taken away about 13 per cent of her lands and population. Ahead

Marches and rallies were a common sight in Weimar Germany. These are the children of the communist party members

lay an unknown but immense amount of war reparation to be paid. The population was sullen, angry and rebellious.

Such, then, was the unhappy state of the world at the time when Hitler received that fateful order to investigate the German Workers' Party.

The Birth of the Nazi Party

Hitler was not impressed by the first meeting of the German Workers' Party which he attended in a Munich beer cellar on 12 September 1919. About two dozen people were scattered around the tables ready for an evening's political discussion. Hitler had gone only to listen, but a suggestion by one man, that Bavaria should join Austria, brought him to his feet. Hitler's reply was so violent that, he claimed, the man left the hall like a 'wet poodle', while the remainder stared at him with 'astonished faces'.

A few days later, he was invited to a committee meeting to be held in a back street beer house. 'I didn't know whether to be angry or laugh', he wrote later. 'I had no intention of joining a ready-made party, but wanted to found one of my own.

33

What they asked me was . . . out of the question.' Eventually, however, out of curiosity, he decided to go. The meeting was held in a dirty gas-lit room at the back of the beer house. Four people were present. He was warmly welcomed into a party which was only forty strong and had about ten shillings in the bank.

Hitler decided to join this unknown group, because here he would have a chance to get control and build up the party to his own design. If he had joined an established party, such as the Nationalists, he would probably have remained a power-less nonentity. It took him two days to make up his mind. Then he joined the committee of the German Workers' Party as its seventh member.

The original committee had few ambitions. They were quite content to remain little more than a club for political discussions. Hitler was not. He began to organise larger meetings and advertise them. Within a month he was attracting audiences of 200. Soon he was put in charge of the Party's propaganda. On 24 February 1920 he held the Party's first mass meeting in the famous Hofbrauhaus beer hall. About 2,000 people attended. Here Hitler renamed the Party the National Socialist German Workers' Party, and attracted considerable attention with the 25-point programme, drawn up in conjunction with two other Party leaders Anton Drexler and Gottfried Feder. This programme became the Nazi creed, and many socialist points were included which gained the support of the working men. Although he declared the 25 points to be unchangeable, 'Hitler's own programme was much simpler, power, power for himself, for the Party, and the Nation with which he identified himself'.[1]

In later years, he quietly dropped the ideas which had served their purpose—gaining him support and power.

‖ THE MEANING OF NAZISM

The first point demanded the union of all Germans into a Greater Germany. Many Germans were now citizens of Austria, Czechoslovakia and Poland. To bring them back into Germany could only be done by force—most probably war.

The second point called for the abolition of the Treaty of

[1] Alan Bullock, *Hitler—a Study in Tyranny*.

Versailles and the Treaty of St Germain which the Allies had made with Austria.

The programme was violently anti-semitic. Jews were to be denied German citizenship. They were not to be allowed to hold public office or to publish newspapers. Those who had entered Germany after World War I were to be expelled.

The socialist points, probably put in at the insistence of Drexler and Feder, help to explain why the Party became so attractive to the working class and the small traders of Germany. These points included the nationalisation of the biggest industries and departmental stores, which, incidentally, were in many cases owned by Jews. The programme also called for the abolition of unearned incomes and ground rents; the confiscation of profits made during the war, and land urgently needed by the State.

In later years when Hitler began to get help from the leading industrialists and landowners, these last points of the programme were to prove embarrassing. Hitler tried to quietly forget them, and of course they were never actually carried out.

THE PARTY BOSS

'After half an hour the applause slowly began to drown the screaming and shouting. . . . When after nearly four hours the hall began to empty, I knew that the principles of the movement which could no longer be forgotten were moving out among the German people.'

These were Hitler's own words in which he described how his 25-point programme was received in the Hofbrauhaus. There is no reason to doubt them. For Hitler was beginning to discover his greatest gift—that of public speaking. Alan Bullock has described Hitler as 'the greatest demagogue[1] in history'. Munich was his training ground: in this city Hitler spoke night after night to audiences ranging from a dozen to several thousand. He learned to contend with shouted interruptions, foot-stamping, mocking laughter or even stony silence. More important, he learned how to catch the attention of his audience, how to read their minds and how to strike them on the raw. His techniques as a speaker were simple.

'The receptive powers of the masses are very restricted and

[1] Demagogue: one who rouses a mob by fiery speeches.

their understanding is feeble. On the other hand, they quickly forget. All effective propaganda must be confined to a few bare necessities and then expressed in a few simple phrases. Only by constantly repeating will you finally succeed in imprinting an idea onto the memory of a crowd. . . . When you lie, tell big lies. This is what the Jews do. The big cheeky lie always leaves traces behind it.'

His choice of words matched his style. Words such as 'smash', 'violent', 'hatred', 'evil' and 'power' appealed to his mass audiences. Not only were audiences lashed in a frenzy by his speeches, but Hitler himself seemed to lose all control. He screamed and spat, waved his arms and rolled his eyes until he was on the verge of hysteria.

Hitler did not rely solely upon words and ideas to win support. He set out to win support through spectacular and dramatic demonstrations of power. The first step was to design an emblem, a party flag, and here he could use his frustrated artistic talent. After many attempts he produced a black *Hakencreuz* (crooked cross), in a white circle upon a red background, an ancient symbol commonly known as the swastika.

Hitler posted ex-servicemen around the halls where he

Nazi Storm-Troopers (SA) parading through Munich

spoke, to silence hecklers (usually Communists). These men were eventually organised into regular strong-arm squads under the disguise of the 'Gymnastic and Sports Division'. Finally in October 1921, they were officially named '*Sturm-abteilung*' (storm-troopers) which was abbreviated to S.A. They were kitted out in brown uniforms and jackboots, and wore swastika armbands. The S.A. 'brownshirts' soon became the most feared men in Germany. Not content with maintaining order at their own meetings, they took to breaking up those of opponents. For taking part in one such raid at the head of his storm-troopers, Hitler received a three months' jail sentence.

The S.A. really made its name a year later, in October 1922, when Hitler took eight hundred of his storm-troopers to a demonstration at Coburg. Kurt Ludecke was at Hitler's side during the march through a hostile crowd:

'The gates were opened against the protests of the now thoroughly alarmed police, and we faced the menacing thousands. With no music, but only drums beating, we marched in the direction of the Schuetzenhalle. We who were in the forefront with Hitler were exposed to very real danger for cobblestones were fairly raining upon us. Sometimes, a man's muscles do his thinking. I sprang from the ranks towards a fellow who was lunging at me with his club uplifted. From behind me my good Ludwig followed. But at the same moment our entire column had turned on our assailants.'

For a quarter-of-an-hour it was a man-to-man battle. At first the police did not take sides, striking at everyone with impartial vigour. 'But soon, probably because they shared our dislike of the street rabble, most of them took our side, and before long we were masters of the field.'[1] Coburg became a Nazi 'battle-honour' and a special medal was given to those who had taken part.

Meanwhile the original members of the Party were becoming unhappy and worried. They did not like the way Hitler was gradually taking over complete control of the Party, nor the direction in which he was steering it. While he was in Berlin during the summer of 1921, they began trying to link up with other similarly-minded political groups. By this they

[1] K. Ludecke, *I knew Hitler.*

hoped to reduce his power because the other group leaders would be more independent.

Hitler returned to Munich and immediately offered to resign. The committee realised that his resignation would mean the end of the Party and refused to accept it. He then demanded complete power in the running of the Party. For a time the Party tried to resist, but it was hopeless. On 21 July 1921 Hitler became the president and absolute leader of the National Socialist German Workers' Party.

HITLER'S CRONIES

During these early days of the Nazi Party, Hitler began to gather round him a number of men, some of whom were eventually to help him to rule Germany, and for a time Europe. You can find further biographies on page 165 of the leading members of Hitler's 'court'.

Captain Ernst Röhm, a tough army officer, was the founder of the S.A. He recruited large numbers of ex-soldiers into the Party. As an army officer he was able to secure a large measure of protection for Hitler and the Nazis. Unfortunately for Röhm, he and Hitler did not see eye to eye on the future of the S.A. Röhm wanted the brownshirts to become regular soldiers; Hitler saw them as political troops. On 30 June 1934 Hitler was to show his gratitude for Röhm's early devotion and service to the Party.

Dietrich Eckhart. If the perverted Röhm was the brawn of the Nazi Party, then Eckhart, until his death through drink in 1923, was the first 'brain'. A journalist by profession, who also wrote poetry and plays, Eckhart, like Hitler, had lived an aimless drifting life. It was Eckhart, also a Jew-hater, who saw in Hitler the raw material of a party leader. During their few years together, Eckhart helped Hitler to improve his knowledge of the German language, lent him books on politics, economics and history, and most important of all, introduced him to many important and wealthy people who would be a great help to him. Hitler called him 'one of the best'.

Alfred Rosenberg was acknowledged as the 'intellectual leader' of the Party. This reputation was mainly based upon his book *The Myth of the Twentieth Century*, a collection of articles and pamphlets dealing with questions of racialism. Rosenberg, also the editor of *Völkischer Beobachter* ('People's Observer'), was a dim-witted man, whose ideas could rarely be understood, let alone put into practice. He ended his life on the gallows at Nuremberg in 1946. (See page 159.)

Rudolf Hess joined the Nazis in 1920 after hearing a speech by Hitler. Born in Egypt, but educated in Germany, Hess had served in the same regiment as Hitler during the war, though they hadn't known each other at the time. Hess eventually became private secretary and a close friend and follower of Hitler for twenty years.

Hermann Göring was the most famous of the early Nazis, for he was a much-decorated fighter pilot of World War I. He married a rich and beautiful Swedish countess in 1920, after which they went to live in Munich. In 1921 Göring met Hitler and joined the Party, making lavish gifts from his wife's fortune. The following year he became Commander of the S.A.

Julius Streicher. In many respects Streicher was the most unpleasant of all the Nazis. He began life as a schoolteacher, but in 1922 became a full-time Nazi. Later, as Nazi boss of Nuremberg, his most revolting speciality became the publishing of a weekly magazine full of filthy stories and 'jokes' attacking the Jews—even other leading Nazis found them sickening, and he was dismissed in 1940. He flogged his victims with a rhinoceros-hide whip, and chased any pretty woman who crossed his path. He was tried at Nuremberg, mumbling that all the judges were Jews, and was dragged to the gallows shouting 'Heil Hitler'. These, then, were some of the strange collection of misfits who first flocked to Hitler's side. Some were outcasts from society, some were failures in their chosen way of life, many were embittered by Germany's defeat in World War I. One thing they had in common was a belief that Nazism was the complete and only answer to their problems. With one or two intelligent exceptions, they all threw their weight behind Hitler in his endeavours to gain control of Germany.

Money Troubles

When in 1921 the amount to be paid in reparations became known—nearly £6,600 million—the German economy rocked.

The value of paper money depends to a large extent on the gold reserves which a country possesses and the confidence which people have in the currency. The German economy was in a battered condition after the war. The mark had steadily been losing value since 1914—this meant that one mark would buy less and less, both at home and abroad. The knowledge that hundreds of millions of pounds worth of Germany's wealth would be pouring out of the country for years ahead completely undermined the currency. As the mark dropped in value, Germany was unable to keep up payments of reparations. The French thought that this was a trick by Germany to escape payments and sent troops into the Ruhr (January 1923). The industrial heart of Germany stopped beating as the miners and the steelworkers went on strike. An undeclared state of war soon existed. French soldiers were attacked and trains carrying coal to France were sabotaged. The French replied by a wave of arrests and even some executions. The steady drop in the value of the mark became a headlong plunge, until it became completely worthless. The American dollar became the measure of value in Germany.

Here is a comparison of values.

Number of marks needed to buy 1 dollar's worth of goods:

1914	4·2
1919	8·9
1921 (Nov.)	70
1922 (Jan.)	192
1922 (Aug.)	1,000
1923 (Jan.)	18,000
1923 (July)	160,000
1923 (Aug.)	1,000,000
1923 (Nov.)	4,200,000,000

Paper money became valueless and bartering of goods the accepted method of trading. Workers were paid daily and spent it as soon as possible after receiving it lest its value should have fallen by the following day. As paper money dropped in value, so more and more was needed until the government had 300 paper-mills and 2,000 printing works on twenty-four-hour shifts to provide it.

WHO GAINED FROM THE INFLATION?

The government was able to pay off its public debts in worthless marks, including war loans of over £2,000 million. The French in the Ruhr, desperately trying to extract reparations, were foiled by the declining mark. The great industrialists were able to pay off all their debts as well. Others borrowed money with which to buy up property and goods at immense profit. Hugo Stinnes became a multi-millionaire in this way; beginning as a steel manufacturer, he soon came to own hotels, newspapers, ships, lorries and timber.

WHO LOST BY THE INFLATION?

The soaring prices completely outstripped wages. A man had to work for ten hours to buy a pound of margarine, and for six weeks to buy a pair of boots! A life-time's savings often became valueless in a matter of weeks. A comfortable pension was insufficient to pay the baker's bill. It was the workers and the middle classes who suffered this economic whirlwind and who became embittered and prepared to listen to words such as Hitler's. 'Believe me', he cried, 'our misery will increase. The scoundrel will get by. The reason: because the State itself has become the biggest swindler and crook. A robber's state! . . . Horrified people notice that they can starve on millions . . . we will no longer submit . . . we want a dictatorship!'

Hitler's Bid for Power

Many people agreed with Hitler. As the financial crisis worsened, and hatred of the Republican Government grew, a plan began to grow in Hitler's mind. The previous year Mussolini's Fascists had marched on Rome during a period of similar disorder in Italy. Mussolini had become Prime Minister as a result. Hitler decided to hold a 'March on Berlin'. The Nazi Party was still too small and unknown to 'go it alone', so Hitler worked hard to gain the support of other anti-republican groups. In February 1923 he succeeded, and the 'Working Union of Patriotic Fighting Associations' was formed. In addition, Hitler tried to get the support of the army. During April he made daily visits to General von Lossow and made several speeches attacking the Republic. 'When we have gained power, we shall have the further duty of taking these creators of ruin, these traitors to their State, and hanging them from the gallows to which they belong.'

In an effort to attract further attention to himself, Hitler decided to use his storm-troopers to break up the annual Trade Union demonstrations on May Day. Many of the 20,000 S.A. parading outside Munich were armed. Hitler and his lieutenants—including Göring, Hess and Himmler, were waiting for a signal from Captain Röhm in the city. The signal never arrived, but Röhm did, unwillingly, and with a large escort of troops and police who quickly surrounded the storm-troopers. Against the advice of some of his lieutenants, Hitler ordered his men to surrender their arms. The whole affair ended in a complete defeat for him.

There were no unpleasant consequences for Hitler, for this was the time of the financial crisis. He did, however, lie low for a few months, only to burst back onto the political scene with even greater vigour.

In September 1923 the government called off the strike in the Ruhr and promised to resume reparation payments. The Nationalists, the Nazis and the Communists joined in a violent attack on the government's decision. The longer the crisis lasted, the greater became the possibility of civil war, and (each hoped) a take-over of the government by themselves.

The Communist threat in Hamburg, Saxony and the Ruhr, was quickly crushed by General von Seeckt, the army commander. The threat from the 'right' came from Bavaria. The Bavarian government, deeply suspicious of Berlin, appointed three men with complete power to carry on the struggle—von Kahr, the State Commissioner; General von Lossow, the local army commander; and Colonel von Seisser, the police chief.

General von Seeckt sacked von Lossow, but the Bavarians ignored the order and made the army swear an oath of loyalty to the Bavarian government. To von Seeckt this was outright rebellion, and he issued a stern warning that any move by the three men would be crushed by force.

Hitler, still urging a 'March on Berlin', was becoming worried. He suspected, rightly, that von Seeckt's warning had been effective. He also realised that as the crisis in the Ruhr was dying down, his chance to act was slipping away. He therefore decided to act on his own initiative, after first getting the army and the police behind him.

THE BEER-HALL PUTSCH[1]

On 6 November a brief notice appeared in a Munich paper. It stated that Commissioner of State Gustav von Kahr was to address a meeting at the Buergerbraukeller—a beer hall on the edge of Munich. Also present would be General von Lossow and Colonel von Seisser. Here was the chance Hitler had been waiting for—to seize the three important men and force them to join the Nazi revolution. The meeting began peaceably enough at 8.30 p.m. Hitler stood quietly beside a pillar with his bodyguard—Ulrich Graf, a butcher and amateur wrestler, and two other Nazis. Then when von Kahr was in the middle of his speech, Göring and a group of armed storm-troopers burst into the hall. Hitler fired a pistol shot into the ceiling and leapt onto the platform. 'The National Revolution', he shouted, 'has begun. There are 600 heavily armed men in the hall. No one may leave. The Bavarian and Reich governments have been removed, and a provisional National Government formed. The army and police are marching on the city under the swastika banner.'

This was one great lie from start to finish, but Hitler hoped that von Kahr and the others would believe it, join him, and make it come true. Under the threat of Hitler's pistol, they promised to join him. By this time General Lüdendorff had arrived, summoned by Hitler to lead the revolution. After much cheering and singing in the hall, Hitler was called away, and the three Bavarian leaders slipped out into the darkness.

By morning, Hitler had nearly 4,000 men in the city, but only the War Ministry buildings had been occupied. In the meantime, von Seeckt had sent a telegram from Berlin ordering von Lossow to crush the rebellion. Von Kahr then announced that the Nazi Party had been dissolved.

The uprising had failed, but, urged on by Lüdendorff, Hitler tried a final desperate gamble. He gathered his men together for a march on Army H.Q. where Lüdendorff was sure the troops would obey him. Shortly after 11 a.m. some

[1] *Putsch*—an attempt to seize power.

3,000 men, led by the General and the ex-corporal, left the Buergerbraukeller, crossed the Ludwig Bridge and headed for the city centre.

The column passed through the first police cordon by threatening to shoot hostages if stopped. The second cordon armed with rifles was drawn up across a narrow street leading onto the Odeonplatz, a broad square. As the Nazi column approached Graf, Hitler's bodyguard, ran up to the police and shouted: 'Don't fire—Lüdendorff and Hitler are coming!'. Then as Hitler shouted out 'Surrender!', the shooting began. The man with whom Hitler was marching arm-in-arm fell

Hitler congratulating the men who marched with him in the Beer-hall Putsch

wounded, dragging him down as well. With a dislocated shoulder, Hitler stumbled to the rear of the column and escaped in a car. Lüdendorff unflinchingly marched on through the police cordon but not one man followed him. The remainder of the column broke and fled leaving nineteen dead behind them, including three policemen.

Two days later Hitler was arrested. He was charged with treason, and his trial began on 26 February 1924. He took full advantage of the opportunities and publicity which the trial gave him. It lasted twenty-four days and received full coverage in German and foreign newspapers. He took full responsibility for the unsuccessful *putsch* and made speech after speech attacking the Republic—the first one lasted four hours. He also made vicious attacks on the chief prosecution witnesses, only General von Lossow standing up to Hitler's jibes. By the end of the trial Hitler had completely dominated the courtroom and become a nationally-known figure. Nevertheless, he received a sentence of five years' imprisonment while Lüdendorff was acquitted.

'MEIN KAMPF'

Hitler served his sentence in the fortress of Landsberg, fifty miles west of Munich. He had a comfortable stay and celebrated his thirty-fifth birthday there. He received parcels and flowers which filled several rooms. There was always a constant stream of visitors to see him, and he was allowed to receive as many books, newspapers and letters as he wished.

One important point became clear to Hitler following the failure of the beer-hall *putsch*. He realised that when he next made a bid for power it must be done legally. The next time he intended to have the army and the police on his side. Hitler's days of rebellion in the streets were over, even though he still intended to win his support in the streets.

During his last five months in prison—he served only nine months of the five-year sentence—Hitler worked on his book. His own title 'Four-and-a-half years struggle against lies, stupidity and cowardice', was changed by his publisher to *Mein Kampf—My Struggle*. The contents matched the original title; hundreds of pages of heavy, long-winded and dull text explaining Hitler's ideas. Although partly autobiographical, it

45

was not at all the racy, exciting exposure which the publisher, Max Amann, had hoped for. Few people in Germany, and even fewer outside, bothered to read it until Hitler had become a world figure and war was approaching. This was a great pity because Hitler had set out quite clearly what he intended to do, and how he planned to do it, when he got into power. Many who did read it, however, refused to take it seriously.

Hitler's Lean Years, 1925–29

LIFE IN WEIMAR GERMANY

The years between Imperial and Nazi rule in Germany (1918–1933) are generally looked upon merely as a period of disorders, strikes and economic problems. The great inflation, the Hitler *putsch*, the 'battle' of Coburg and the depression of the early 1930s are the best-remembered episodes. Such memories do much to paint a picture of gloom. It is also true that these years saw a slackening of the accepted moral codes. Large cities such as Berlin and Munich were notorious for scandals and vice of every kind. Alcoholism, gambling, drug taking and even black magic attracted hundreds of people. The German film industry, second largest in the world to Hollywood, glamorised

A street brawl between rival political groups, 1929

Man shitting himself

this low type of life. Films of violence, passion, crime and sentimentality were churned out rapidly and enjoyed considerable popularity. A best-selling book of this time, Oswald Spengler's *Decline of the West*, also encouraged this 'eat, drink and be merry' attitude. Spengler painted a picture of the world as a meaningless jungle in which the 'young' German nation would nevertheless triumph.

The brutal street fights, the 376 political murders which stained the first four years of the Republic's history, and the provocative speeches of men like Hitler all combined to lessen public respect for law and order. Few Germans could feel secure during a period when there was a general election on average once every fifteen months and a change of Cabinet once every eight.

This, however, is a very one-sided picture of Weimar Germany. There is no denying the very real misery brought to millions of Germans by the inflation of 1923, and during the depression years after 1930. But the middle years of the Weimar Republic (1924–29) saw considerable advances in most walks of life. Loans from America totalling several thousand million dollars poured into Germany. Little of it was ever repaid. These loans enabled German industry to be thoroughly modernised, and in coal and steel the production figures for 1928 showed an increase of 120 per cent on those for 1913. The building industry flourished, over 300,000 houses and flats being built each year in the late 1920s. Complaints were in fact raised by the Treasury that too much was being spent on roads, swimming pools, parks, libraries and sports arenas. The health insurance programme was extended to cover over 20 million people. In spite of all the economic crises, the Trade Union movement managed to secure an eight-hour working day, at least in principle. Two new universities were built, at Hamburg and Cologne, lasting monuments to a period of great intellectual achievement. Distinguished names are recorded in every field: men such as Paul Klee (painting), Paul Hindemith (music), Gustav Meyer (history), and the writers Bertolt Brecht and Thomas Mann. Most famous of all was Albert Einstein, the brilliant physicist, who was to spend his last years in the U.S.A. As a Jew, he had to flee from Nazi Germany.

William L. Shirer, author of *Berlin Diary* and the immense *Rise and Fall of the Third Reich*, was a young journalist in 1925 when he first arrived in Germany. In the following passage taken from the latter book he gives his impressions of the life and spirit of Germany at that time.

'I was stationed in Paris and occasionally London at that time, and fascinating as they were to a young American, they paled a little when one came to Berlin and Munich. A wonderful ferment was working in Germany. Life seemed more free, more modern, more exciting than any place I had ever seen. Nowhere did the arts or intellectual life seem so lively. In contemporary writing, painting, architecture, in music and drama, there were new currents and new talents. And everywhere the accent was on youth. One sat up with young people all night in the pavement cafes, the plush bars, the summer camps, on a Rhineland steamer or in a smoke-filled artist's studio and talked endlessly about life. They were a healthy, carefree, sun-worshipping lot and they were filled with an enormous zest for living to the full and in complete freedom. The old oppressive Prussian spirit seemed dead and buried'.

Hitler also enjoyed those days.

'I used to spend the day in leather shorts. In the evening I would put on a dinner jacket and tails or go to the opera. We made excursions by car . . . my supercharged Mercedes was a joy to all. Afterwards we would prolong the evening in the company of actors either at the Theatre restaurant or on a visit to the Berneck. . . . From all points of view, these were marvellous days.'

But Nazism was not making headway, so Hitler could not afford to rest.

PROSPECTS OF PEACE

Germany, under the guidance of Gustav Stresemann, the Foreign Secretary, was now on better terms with the Great Powers. In the early days of the Weimar Republic she had been thrust into the arms of the other great outcast Soviet Russia. With a new stable currency in Germany, Stresemann was able to persuade Britain, France and the U.S.A. to work a new scheme for the payment of war damages. The Dawes plan, by which payments would be fixed from year to year, was agreed upon with much relief. The Locarno pact was signed in 1925, Germany agreeing to respect existing frontiers in the west and not to go to war to change them. Following this in 1926 Germany was admitted to the League of Nations, and in 1928 fifteen nations including Germany signed the Kellogg pact renouncing war as a means of achieving their aims and ambitions.

Meanwhile the veteran Field-Marshal Hindenburg had become President of the Weimar Republic so that its status at home and abroad stood at its highest point. The election of Hindenburg showed that most Germans still preferred the old pre-1918 type of government. Hindenburg, a conservative Field-Marshal, was much preferred to any Republican candidate. He was an honourable man and loyal to the Weimar Republic. Hitler was now certain that violent revolution was not the way to power. He was determined that he must become Chancellor of Germany legally, with the Nazi Party democratically elected.

While Hitler was in prison Germany began to recover her economic strength. The French left the Ruhr, the U.S.A. began to invest money in Germany and the new currency, the '*Rentenmark*', was confidently accepted. Nazism, which bred on disorder and unrest, was leaderless and began to break into splinter groups. Some Nazis wanted to join with other parties, some even took part in the scorned Reichstag elections, while Ernst Röhm began to weld the S.A. (storm-troopers) into a tough fighting force which he hoped would become the new German army. 'By the end of Hitler's year in prison these quarrels and dissensions had reached such a pitch that it appeared possible to write off the former Nazi Party as a serious force in German or Bavarian politics.'[1]

Hitler probably encouraged these quarrels so that no one could take over control whilst he was in prison. They continued after his release at Christmas 1924, and many of the 'old guard' left the Party. With the few faithful members that were left Hitler held a mass meeting in February 1925, at which he was so well received that the authorities in every German state banned him from public speaking for over two years.

[1] Bullock, *op. cit.*

The Nazis rapidly lost support as unemployment declined and a temporary prosperity returned. Soon after Hitler was imprisoned in 1924 an election was held and the Nazis gained thirty-two seats. Another election coincided with Hitler's release and this time the Nazis gained only fourteen seats. Four years later their total had dropped to twelve. This evident failure was a severe test for Hitler's position.

HITLER'S LEADERSHIP

Hitler never lost confidence in himself, but others did and so he found himself engaged in a struggle for the leadership of the Party. The top Nazis from North Germany disagreed with him about the fate of former royal property in Germany. At a meeting they not only voted against Hitler but supported a brand new Nazi programme. Hitler called his own meeting, spoke for two hours and won over the two leading North Germans.

Other Nazis disliked the amount of Party money which Hitler spent on himself, including running a large Mercedes-Benz, but the biggest challenge was from the S.A. The new Commander, Captain von Salomon, refused to knuckle under to Hitler's command. The S.A. still continued to 'play at soldiers' and generally go its own way. Hitler answered by founding his own hand-picked force, the S.S. (see page 73). Membership of the Party grew from 27,000 in 1925 to 72,000 in 1927 and 178,000 by 1929. Considering that the adult male population of Germany was over 20 million, Hitler was far from satisfied.

THE ORGANISATION OF THE PARTY

In preparation for the day when he would have complete power, Hitler began a careful organisation of the Party. The country was first divided into *Gaus*, or districts—thirty-four in all—under the command of Gauleiters. *Gaus* were subdivided in *Kreis*, which in turn contained several *Ortsgruppen*. An *Ortsgruppe* usually covered one city, and within each there were further subdivisions to cover each street and block of flats. Hitler also appointed a 'shadow cabinet' to be prepared to take over the government. The propaganda machine, which launched vicious attacks on the Republic, he directed himself.

To promote these attacks the Nazis were already running three newspapers.

Shortage of money was always a problem. Members paid subscriptions, and collections were taken at meetings, but it was from the directors of great industries that the real money came. The Communists were an active and vigorous organisation in Germany in the 1920s, and there were many fierce street battles between the Nazi storm-troopers and the Communist *Rotfrontkämpferbund* ('Red Front Fighters'). Hitler's fierce speeches against the Communists were to win him the approval and help of businessmen who feared nationalisation of their firms.

The Great Depression

Hitler was still making little headway. In the words of Alan Bullock, he was still 'a small-time politician little known outside the South and even there regarded as part of the lunatic fringe of Bavarian politics'. Finally in 1929 fortune began to favour him. Yet another committee had met to discuss Germany's payment of reparations. In June 1929 their findings were published as the Young Plan, which required Germany to pay a much smaller sum annually for 59 years! Also the Allied forces were to leave the Rhineland. Four months later Gustav Stresemann, the man who had done so much to raise

Many women lost their jobs in the Great Depression

German prestige abroad, died. Three weeks after his death the stock market on New York's Wall Street crashed. Shares which had been worth a fortune became valueless overnight. The stream of American loans and investments into Germany abruptly dried up. Repayment of old loans became due and the German economy began to crack. World trade sagged and factories and mines closed. Germany's unemployment figures began to climb rapidly from 1,320,000 in September 1929 to 3 million in September 1930, and over 4 million a year later.

At such a desperate time as this for Germany Hitler found a powerful ally in Alfred Hugenburg, owner of a chain of newspapers and cinemas. Hugenburg hated the Weimar Republic, the Treaty of Versailles and the Trade Unions. He offered Hitler all his support in a campaign against the Young Plan. Almost overnight Hitler became a nationally known figure. His speeches were widely reported and read. Contributions began to pour into the Nazi Party Treasury. The Young Plan was passed but in the increasing misery of the depression an increasing number of ears turned to Hitler.

THE APPEAL OF NAZISM

The combination of 'Nationalist' and 'Socialist' was one of the Party's big advantages. The Nationalist Party consisting mainly of ex-officers, businessmen and landowners could not hope to attract the workers. The Communists on the other hand had attracted only disgruntled and active workers. Taking orders from Moscow—the international headquarters of Communism—the Communist leaders were not in a position to use Germany's damaged pride to advantage.

Hitler claimed an interest in, and therefore, the attention of, all classes of German society. To the army he promised expansion and rearmament, to businessmen he promised large orders and the crushing of Communists who wanted nationalisation; to the unemployed he promised work; to the middle classes, ruined by the inflation and the depression, he promised to root out the cause of their misery—the Jews and the 'money barons'. To the Nationalists he promised an end to the Treaty of Versailles. He still chanted out meaningless socialist catch-phrases to attract working men, but he had no intention of fulfilling them.

The success of these 'something-for-everyone' promises was dramatically illustrated at the general election of September 1930. Unemployment was rising, and Germany was committed to paying reparation to the French for over half a century. The frail prosperity of the last five years had suddenly disappeared and the German people were bitter and disappointed.

Hitler began a vigorous campaign of speeches, rallies and marches. His posters screamed out promises and made violent attacks upon the 'enemies' of the country. At the major rallies, the Nazis used every trick they could to win support. In one of the new stadiums, 100,000 people would be gathered awaiting the arrival of the Party leader. Suddenly, they would all lean forward and the word passed 'Hitler is coming . . . Hitler is here—Heil Hitler!' A fanfare of trumpets would sound and the cheering begin. Hitler, dressed in his storm-trooper's uniform, would march smartly out into the centre of the arena, his arm held aloft in the Nazi salute.

Then the speech would begin. For two hours or more Hitler would promise and plead, rant and rave, curse and cajole, his words echoing like a whiplash around the cheering thousands. When at last he had finished, he would climb into his huge black open Mercedes-Benz. Then once again giving the outstretched arm salute, he would be carried out of the stadium amidst a final roar of cheers.

As the car left a torchlight procession of several hundred S.S. men would march in whilst fireworks broke overhead. Then massed bands struck up and the whole assembly joined in the singing of '*Deutschland über Alles*' [1] and (in later years) the 'Horst Wessel Song'.[2]

These openly violent and spectacular methods of the Nazis drew many supporters. Some were attracted by the uniforms, badges and banners, particularly the ex-soldiers. Many were impressed by what seemed to be the irresistible force of the S.A. The S.A. was an omen of Germany's recovery. Supporters of the other parties probably watched the Nazi show of force and realised that if 'you can't beat 'em, join 'em'. Many

---

[1] 'Germany above all.'

[2] Horst Wessel was a young S.A. man killed during a street fight with the Communists in 1931. He rapidly became a Nazi martyr.

others who were repelled by Nazism must, quite naturally, have been frightened into silence and inactivity by Nazi brutalities.

Whatever the mixed feelings of the German population, Hitler believed that the S.A. was his trump card. He went out of his way to encourage their activities, and glorify as heroes those members who were killed or wounded.

When the votes had been counted, it was found that the Nazis had increased their number of seats from 12 to 107. This made them the second largest party in Germany. New members flocked to join the Party, and membership of the S.A. rose to half a million. As the depression deepened, tension increased in Germany, and vicious street fights took place. All

Hitler Youth, banned from wearing uniforms and badges, marching through Berlin, 1930

the leading parties had their private armies. In addition to the S.A. there was the Nationalist *Stahlhelm* (steel helmet), the Socialist *Reichbanner* and the Communist *Rotfrontkämpferbund*.

Berlin, the Prussian capital, was a Communist stronghold, but the Nazis were determined to gain control of it. The

54

Party leader in Berlin was Joseph Goebbels, a Doctor of Philosophy, and a cripple. The situation had become so lawless that the Prussian government forbade the Nazis to wear their uniforms in public. While the storm-troopers were doing their best in the streets to destroy the Republic, the newly elected Nazi deputies were trying just as hard in the Reichstag. They marched in wearing full uniform, joking, shouting and singing. Interruptions, points of order and petty discussions brought debates and legislation almost to a halt. Not to be outdone, the Communists also joined in. Eventually, on 31 March 1931 the Reichstag adjourned for seven months.

THE NAZI BREAK-THROUGH

Sensing that the Republic was mortally wounded, the extreme right wing joined up for the kill. A meeting in October 1930 led to the formation of the Harzburg Front. Hitler was there, of course, and the wealthy Hugenburg; Franz Seldte, leader of the *Stahlhelm*, Dr Schacht, head of the Reichsbank, and Fritz Thyssen, President of Vereinigte Stahlwerke (United Steel Works), the largest steel combine in Europe.

Through the support of such powerful and wealthy men, Hitler was invited to make a speech at the Industry Club in Düsseldorf. In a long speech, he launched a violent attack upon the Communists and the Weimar Government. He was given a long applause by the assembled businessmen, and soon large contributions to the Party funds began to arrive.

Throughout 1931 the depression continued and such was the support gained by the Nazis that Hitler agreed to try to oppose Hindenburg for the Presidency in April 1932. Although Hindenburg won with nearly 19 million votes, Hitler gained over 13 million, and Thalmann, the Communist, less than 4 million. This showed that a Government acceptable to Hitler was necessary if civil war was to be avoided. Therefore, Chancellor Brüning, who was ruling by Decree, and had banned the S.A. and the S.S., was forced to resign. Hindenburg appointed Franz von Papen to be Chancellor with a 'non-party' Government, but the Reichstag refused to support it, so another general election was arranged for 31 July, 1932. The S.A., which had been previously dissolved, when found to be mixed up in revolutionary plots, was allowed to re-form. In return,

Hitler promised support for von Papen. In Berlin alone, 82 people were killed and 400 seriously wounded in political riots during the two months before the election. The worst incidents took place in Hamburg in July, when Nazi marchers were fired upon from the roof-tops by Communists; nineteen deaths and 300 injuries were reported.

Nazi preparations for the election were at their best. Parades, posters, the press, mass meetings and speeches, all helped to drive home the Hitler message. Leading Nazi speakers criss-crossed Germany by plane, train and car to reach every corner. One crowd of many thousands waited in pouring rain for Hitler until 2.30 in the morning! Such was the support for Hitler all over Germany for when the results were announced it was found that the Nazis had doubled their poll in two years, securing 13,745,000 votes (230 seats out of 608). The Social Democrats were second with 8 million (133 seats), and the Communists a poor third. This meant that no government could rule unless Hitler supported it. The time had come for him to move into power.

THE CRUCIAL WEEKS—NOVEMBER 1932–JANUARY 1933

Von Papen had no intention of letting Hitler into office, except in a minor capacity, but hoped to force him to come to terms by keeping him 'on edge'. Hitler tried to ally with the Centre Party but von Papen dissolved Parliament and yet another election was imminent. This time the Nazis were short of money but Hitler's iron determination held firm. He refused to come to terms with anyone and although the Nazis lost thirty-four seats and the Communists gained eleven, the Nazis were still the largest party in Parliament. Von Papen was delighted to see Hitler lose votes. Other members of the cabinet, worried by the success of the Communists and even the possibility of civil war, forced von Papen to resign. Old Field-Marshal Hindenburg called Hitler to the palace on 19 November, but Hitler refused to become Chancellor unless given very great powers. Hindenburg refused and reappointed von Papen, whereupon General von Schleicher declared that the army could not maintain order if the worst happened. The 'worst' would be an attack by Poland combined with a general strike and a rising by the Nazis and Communists. Faced with such a fearful (and unreal) prospect Hindenburg was forced to change his mind and on 2 December General Kurt von Schleicher became Chancellor of Germany. His term of office was destined to last only fifty-nine days.

HITLER CLINCHES A DEAL

Von Schleicher had to produce a government which would have the support of all the right-wing and centre parties, including the Nazis. Hitler had no intention of supporting von Schleicher even though the Nazi Party was having serious money troubles. Von Schleicher was also unsuccessful with the Social Democrats, but his position was still quite strong, while the Nazis seemed to be slipping.

Then Hitler's luck turned. He received a secret request from von Papen for a meeting. He caught the night train to Bonn and continued the journey to Cologne by car, changing vehicles on the way to throw off pursuers. The two leaders finally agreed to work for the overthrow of von Schleicher. Von Papen did not discount the idea of becoming Chancellor himself, and he still believed the Nazis could be kept in check by various safeguards. Von Schleicher meanwhile had been forced to admit to President Hindenburg that he could not secure a parliamentary majority. When von Papen offered to provide an alternative government Hindenburg agreed and von Schleicher had to resign. This alternative government was to be a coalition of Nazis and Nationalists with Hitler as Chancellor. Although this coalition did not have a majority, Hitler knew that it would have after another election, so to break the deadlock he agreed to become Chancellor and thus came into power legally. This was the only way in which a 'popular' government could be formed, otherwise there was the possibility of a violent revolution.

On the morning of 30 January 1933 Hitler received a summons from President Hindenburg. After thirteen years of struggle Adolf Hitler had become Chancellor of Germany.

WHY THE WEIMAR REPUBLIC FAILED

Upon the evening of Hitler's appointment, the Nazis held a huge torchlight procession through Berlin. The streets were jammed with cheering thousands. High on a balcony above Wilhelmstrasse stood the tall and still erect figure of the eighty-four-year-old President Paul von Hindenburg. Beside him, with outstretched arm, the ex-corporal and now Chancellor of Germany, Adolf Hitler, gazed down at the funeral procession of the Weimar Republic.

For the Weimar Republic had 'died' over two years before. In September 1930, the three extremist parties (Nazis, Nationalists and Communists) had gained the same number of seats as the two mainstay parties of the Republic (Social Democrats and Centre). Brüning, Chancellor from March 1930 to May 1932, had been able to govern only by use of the Presidential Decree (Article 48 of the Weimar Constitution). The use of the Decree, which by-passed the Reichstag, paved the way for Hitler's rule: many of his early methods and measures came as no great shock to the Germans.

The Weimar Republic collected enemies right from its birth. The Nazis and Nationalists made no secret of their destructive plans. Even the Communists worked hard to wreck the left-wing government. They mocked the Social Democrats, calling them 'Social Fascists', and even joined forces with the Nazis in a transport strike in Berlin. Throughout the fourteen years of its existence, the Republic had a hard core of some seven million voters, who never wavered in their support. Many workers did, however, backslide into the Communists' ranks, and even more crossed into the Nazi camp as the unemployment situation worsened. The middle classes, embittered by inflation and frightened by the growing power of the Trade Unions and Communists, also turned to Hitler.

The scales were heavily weighted against the Republic. The early attacks of the right and left wing extremists forced it to turn to the army for support. Weimar politicians had signed the Treaty of Versailles; they had allowed the French to occupy the Ruhr, and they were unable to stop the political street battles. The mental image created for a great many Germans was of a weak and treacherous government which was preventing Germany from becoming a first-rate power again. To such people Hitler's promises sounded doubly tempting. Weak as it was, the Weimar Republic was the first attempt to give Germany a democratic government. This freedom was something new to Germany, which in the past had always accepted the strict rule of one man or a one-leader party. Now it had gone to the opposite extreme with eight squabbling minority parties. Britain had taken hundreds of years including a civil war to develop her parliamentary system. To expect Germany to achieve the same in ten years was expecting the impossible, especially at a time of economic crisis. It was economic troubles which fertilised the seeds of Nazism. The hungry, the ruined, the unemployed and the misfits, all blamed their troubles upon the Weimar Government. These were the people who turned a ready ear to Hitler's promises and helped to lift him to power.

The Character and Private Life of Adolf Hitler

Hitler's personal tastes and habits were surprisingly simple. Power was his greatest satisfaction. There was no limit to his ambitions. We have seen how he made himself complete master of the Nazi movement. Step by step he was to become master of Germany, and in 1938 he began his campaign to overrun Europe. Yet for a man who achieved so much, starting from nothing, Hitler was lazy. He never had a steady job and tended to become easily bored. Even his long ranting speeches were often prepared in a hurry shortly before he delivered them. He was helped by a fantastic memory and could reel off long lists of facts and figures with very little effort. He often did this to cover up his ignorance in front of experts.

When not attending rallies and conferences, Hitler loved to sit down with a bunch of cronies and talk. It is easy to guess who did most of the talking, and sometimes their get-togethers lasted until 3 a.m. Such was his nervous energy that he never needed alcohol, tobacco or coffee to keep him going. Neither would he eat meat, but he enjoyed cream cakes and chocolates. For relaxation he loved to listen to the music of Wagner and some of Beethoven's works. He also enjoyed fast drives in his chauffeur-driven Mercedes-Benz. He hardly ever took physical exercise. This way of life affected his health and he became very worried about it. He began to seek out strange remedies, eventually turning to drugs, including pep pills and tranquillisers.

Women were generally attracted to Hitler, and he liked to be surrounded by pretty ones. He seemed to regard them as decorations and did not approve of women who thought for themselves. As far as we know, there were only two women in his life. In 1928 he fell in love with his niece, Geli Raubal, and was heartbroken when she committed suicide in 1931. Soon after her death he met Eva Braun, a pretty, empty-headed blonde. During Hitler's years in power Eva stayed out of sight, but she joined him for his final days. According to a German doctor, Hans-Dietrich Roehrs, in a book published in 1965, Eva may have had two children by Hitler, born in 1941 and 1943.

Although brought up a Catholic, Hitler soon abandoned all religion. He admired the organisation of the Church, but regarded Christianity as fit only for slaves. Pity, humanity and conscience were signs of weakness to Hitler and throughout his life he never showed mercy to a man who crossed his path. He believed that anything could be achieved if one was determined enough, if one had sufficient willpower. On many occasions, he gave remarkable demonstrations of this willpower. When the tide seemed to be running against him, when lesser men cautioned retreat, Hitler stood firm. At first it brought him remarkable successes, but in his last years when he should have given way and retreated he refused. Unable to bend, he broke.

2 Hitler's Germany: 1933–39

Der Führer (The Leader)

Having become Chancellor with only 37 per cent of the votes cast, Hitler wanted fresh elections to be held, hoping to impress or terrify more people into voting for the Nazis. Meanwhile he joined forces with the right-wing Nationalist Party (army officers, factory owners and landowners) and set out to smear the Communists, his bitterest enemies, at the Reichstag Fire Trial.

On the night of 27 February 1933 the Reichstag (Parliament) building was destroyed by fire, and the police captured, redhanded, a young Dutch Communist, Marinus van der Lubbe. The Nazis proclaimed this to be part of a vast international plot and put the Communist leaders on trial. Göring was prosecutor, but only van der Lubbe was found guilty and many people believed the Nazis had started the fire themselves in order to 'frame' the Communists.

When the new elections were held after weeks of vast meetings and parades the Nazis were disappointed to gain only 43·9 per cent of the total votes cast. But with their allies the Nationalists they had a small majority. When the Communists were forbidden to take their seats the Nazis had an absolute majority (more than half) of the seats.

Results of the Reichstag elections—5 March 1933:

Nazis	17,277,200	votes
Social Democrats	7,181,600	,,
Communists	4,848,100	,,
Centre Party	4,424,900	,,
Nationalists	3,136,800	,,

Within a month of the election, Hitler secured the passing of a law which was to be the foundation stone of his tyranny. This so-called 'Enabling Law' transferred that power of making laws from the Reichstag to the Cabinet which meant, in effect, Hitler.

Reichchancellor Adolf Hitler takes the salute of the German Army

Ok, who nicked the tray!

Only the Social Democrats resisted this bill, probably because Hitler had promised the other parties that he would not misuse this power; but the voting was four to one in favour of this 'Enabling Law' and so the way was now open for the Nazis to take control of all Germany.

DESTRUCTION OF THE OPPOSITION

The Trade Unions. The first major victim of the Nazis was the vast and powerful German Trade Union movement. It was a possible breeding ground for Socialism and Communism, and therefore opposition to Hitler. On 2 May 1933 scores of Trade Union leaders were arrested and beaten up. Their offices were looted and all their funds and property seized. A Nazi-led 'Labour Front' was established to control the workers and ensure peace in factories and workshops.

The other political parties. A week after the destruction of the Trade Unions the Social Democratic Party suffered a similar fate, soon to be followed by the Communists. All their property, possessions and funds were seized and both parties were banned. The Centre Party, which had supported Hitler in return for vague promises, collapsed in July 1933, along with the few others still remaining.

62

Less than six months after becoming Chancellor Hitler was able to pass a law which stated that the Nazis were to be the only political party allowed in Germany. The penalty for breaking this law was three years' imprisonment.

To draw all Germany further under Nazi control Hitler abolished local state parliaments (very roughly equivalent to English County Councils). He replaced them by a governor, who in most cases was the Nazi Party chief for the area.

THE NIGHT OF THE LONG KNIVES

The huge S.A. organisation, on whose shoulders Hitler had grappled his way to power, was becoming a serious embarrassment now that its main task had been completed. The rank-and-file were mostly unemployed when not fighting for the Nazi cause. Now they expected that with Hitler in command they would be given soft jobs with power and privileges. Not even Hitler could provide two or three million such jobs. Nor was he willing for several reasons to agree to the plan of the S.A. Commander, Ernst Röhm, to turn the S.A. into a new Reichswehr (Regular Army). Many S.A. men wanted to see Germany's heavy industries taken over by the State and here again Hitler was in complete disagreement with them.

As the months passed tension increased between the S.A. leaders and the Nazis' leaders and for Hitler there was only one answer to the problem. At 3 o'clock on the morning of 30 June 1934 squads of S.S. men (Hitler's special guard units) swooped on everyone considered to be a real or possible enemy of Hitler and shot them after one-minute 'Trials'.

Amongst the leading victims were:
Ernst Röhm and three *Obergruppenführer* (major-generals) of the S.A.
Erich Klausner and Adelbert Probst—leaders of the Catholic Action and Catholic Youth Organisation.
Gregor Strasser, former first assistant to Hitler.
General von Bredow—leading army officer.
General von Schleicher—former Chancellor.
One tragic victim was music critic Willi Schmidt, taken by mistake for Willi Schmidt, S.A. leader.
Oberleutnant Schultz, Strasser's right-hand man, was 'taken for a ride' in a car by S.S. men. On reaching a deserted stretch

63

of road Schultz was roughly bundled out of the car. 'Now run, you swine', shouted the S.S. commander. Schultz set off down the road, but before he had gone a dozen yards the S.S. men opened fire. He collapsed into a heap with five bullet wounds. The S.S. men then drove off leaving him to die in a great pool of blood. But Schultz, who had been wounded fifteen times in World War I, was a tough nut. Presently a horrified driver pulled up and rushed him to a doctor. Schultz made a miraculous recovery and later escaped to Switzerland.

Hitler tried to 'whitewash' the massacres when he spoke in the Reichstag on 13 July by claiming he had saved Germany from a violent revolution. In fact he was showing that opposition to his plans was fatal. (Röhm was on holiday and fast asleep when arrested!) He admitted that 77 people had died but the number may have been as high as 400.

Less than a month later President Hindenburg died and Hitler took over his position, thus becoming Head of State and Commander-in-Chief of the Armed Forces as well as Chancellor and Chief of the Nazi Party, a tremendous concentration of power. When asked to vote on Hitler's action 38 million Germans expressed themselves in favour.

The Nazi Stranglehold

Many wise and important men who visited Germany in the 1930s were impressed by Hitler's achievements. Sir Arnold Wilson, M.P., spoke on the BBC after his visit to Germany in May 1934. 'I have seen German youth displaying in work and play an energy and enthusiasm which, because it is wholly unselfish, is wholly good.' Unlike Soviet Russia, visitors could wander freely around the country (apart from certain military areas). Most agreed that the people, especially the young, seemed proud, keen and unafraid. Hitler had wiped out the shame of the past, particularly the defeat of 1918, and had given back Germany her strength and pride.

Behind this happy face which Germany showed to the world the Nazi leaders were ruthlessly reshaping the country to Hitler's vision, 'nazifying' institutions and attacking those who would not fit into the Nazi State. Germany was being trained and prepared for the struggle which lay ahead.

THE JEWS

The first and foremost Nazi victims were Germany's half-million Jews, members of a race which has been persecuted for nearly 2,000 years but which in 1933 was on the threshold of a plot to exterminate it completely.

Hitler's hatred for the Jews now knew no bounds; words like 'deadly poison', 'vermin', 'abscess' and 'parasite' used in reference to the Jews crop up in almost every speech and every chapter of his books. In 1945 he talked of the British as a 'Jew-rotted race', the worst insult he believed he could throw.

Writing of Hitler's anti-semitism (hatred of the Jews) Alan Bullock says: 'To read these pages (of Hitler's book, *Mein Kampf*) is to enter a world of insane, a world peopled by hideous and distorted shadows. The Jew is no longer a human being, he has become a mythical figure, a grimacing, leering devil invested with infernal powers, the incarnation of evil.'

Hitler wasted no time; in June 1933 Jews were banned from holding positions of importance such as in the civil service, broadcasting, newspapers, education and entertainment. In 1935 they were deprived of German citizenship and forbidden to marry non-Jews (the Nuremberg Laws).

Meanwhile a more sinister campaign had begun to make their lives as miserable as possible. Signs began to appear outside shops and even towns refusing them admittance. On one dangerous bend a sign was erected—'Germans: slow—Jews: 70 m.p.h.' Jewish shops were labelled and guarded by S.A. men to bar customers from entering. By 1936 half the Jews in Germany were without means of support while all were finding it increasingly difficult to get even food, clothing and medicines.

A steady stream of Jews began pouring out of the country to seek refuge abroad but thousands more were already beginning to fill the concentration camps (see page 78) specially built for Hitler's 'enemies'.

The fiercest attack on Germany's Jewish population in this period before the war came in November 1938, the 'Week of Broken Glass' after a young Jew shot a German embassy official in Paris; by way of revenge a fine of 1,000 million marks was levied on the German Jewish population, about

Storm-troopers picketing a Jewish shop

7,000 of their shops were looted and many savage beatings-up took place. Fritz Schurrman was one of the 20,000 Jews arrested that week. He was thrown into a cell with three others, one of whom was a soldier. They nervously discussed their possible fate but they did not have long to wait. At midnight they were aroused, herded outside and given three slices of bread each. They were then packed into open lorries and driven without coats, through the freezing night.

Eventually they arrived at a station with 800 others and were packed into cattle wagons. Many were in a state of exhaustion and collapse. A Jewish lawyer lay on the platform. He had been badly disabled by war injuries, having lost an eye, a hand, a foot, his nose and part of his skull which had been replaced by a silver plate.

An S.S. man was clubbing him with a rifle butt and shouting 'If he doesn't get up now, he'll stay there for good!' Eventually the lawyer was dragged into the wagon by his fellow victims and the train headed for the concentration camp.

But far worse was yet to come.

THE CHRISTIAN CHURCHES

Nazism and Christianity were almost completely opposed to

each other; the one based on blind obedience to Hitler and a brotherhood of Germanic races, with violence and hatred to other races and nations. The other teaching the brotherhood of *all* men, charity, and pity for the weak and helpless.

If Germany were to be completely 'nazified' then Hitler realised he must wipe out Christianity. Here lay his greatest problem; one which he failed to solve in the time he had available, in spite of the most strenuous efforts.

THE ROMAN CATHOLIC CHURCH

With its large membership, strong discipline and efficient organisation, the Catholic Church in Germany was one of Hitler's principal targets. Although he soon made a Concordat (agreement) with the Pope to protect the Catholic Church in Germany, the attack actually began within ten days of the signing when the Catholic Youth League was broken up. Catholic schools were changed into Nazi schools where religious teaching was banned. Children were taught to 'worship' Hitler and encouraged to break the laws of God and the Church.

The Nazi magazines *Das Schwarze Korps* and *Der Sturmer* kept up a flood of anti-Christian stories, songs, poems and cartoons designed to bring dishonour on the Church. 'Rome for the Priests — Palestine for Jews — Germany for the Germans' was a popular slogan of the time. Others are not fit to print here.

The greatest possible publicity was given to the trials of clergy accused of smuggling money out of Germany for missionary work abroad. In many cases physical violence was inflicted, as in the case of Father Kravasnik, who was hurled out of a window of a house in Vienna, breaking both his legs.

The most outspoken critics of the Nazis were Cardinal Faulhaber of Munich and Bishop von Galen of Münster. Both managed to avoid the arrest and imprisonment which befell many lesser clergymen.

THE PROTESTANT CHURCHES

In July 1933 Hitler established a 'Reich Church' under Ludwig Müller with the intention of uniting all Germany's Protestant Churches under Nazi control. After a typical Nazi terror campaign the ministers were slowly forced to submit, but with increasing opposition. Led by Pastor Martin Niemöller (a submarine commander in World War I), a group of clergymen formed the Confessional Church to oppose the Nazis. After being acquitted of treason Niemöller was thrown into a concentration camp where he remained until 1945.

The Confessional Church remained a powerful force in Germany throughout Hitler's reign; the 'Reich Church' had failed to take over Protestantism. Christianity had proved the strongest defence against the brutal strength of Nazism.

EMPLOYMENT AND THE WORKING-MEN

The promise of 'work for all' which Hitler had made when campaigning for election in 1932 was a promise rapidly fulfilled. Upon taking office as Chancellor in 1933 Hitler had the task of finding 6 million new jobs; by 1936 he had found 5 million; by 1939 Germany was actually short of labour.

The work which Hitler provided was centred on the rebuilding of Germany's armed forces. Compulsory military service and the manufacturing of large numbers of aeroplanes,

Young Germans doing six months' compulsory service in the Labour Corps

A hundred and twenty thousand men were employed on building motor-ways across Germany in the 1930s

tanks, artillery and submarines quickly reduced the number of unemployed after 1935. School-leavers spent six months in labour camps doing agricultural and forestry work while thousands of other men were employed on the construction of fine new buildings and the impressive autobahns (motorways) which swept for hundreds of miles across Germany.

Family allowances were paid to encourage married women to give up paid jobs (which were quickly filled by men) and of course the unfortunate inmates of concentration camps were not listed as unemployed. The Nazi Party itself was a fountain of new jobs as it duplicated every government department and there was no shortage of recruits for the S.S. (see page 73).

At a time when Britain and other Western nations were grappling unsuccessfully with the 'Great Depression' (a standstill in trade meaning great unemployment), Germany was enjoying a 'boom' period.

One of Hitler's first acts, as we read on page 62, was to smash Trade Unionism. The new 'Labour Front' provided no protection for the working-men as wages and hours of work

69

were controlled by the government. Strikes were forbidden, wages were low and hours of work long; every worker had to pay into funds of various kinds. It was not easy to change jobs as the employer kept each man's 'workbook' containing a full 'record of his life'. (Without this workbook, a man could not get a job.)

The fact that Hitler had kept his promise and provided work after the misery of the dole queues must have been one reason why the workers of Germany were prepared to lose their freedom. To some extent they looked on Hitler and the Nazis as saviours.

Germany's businessmen were highly pleased by Hitler's industrial programme. Freed from the opposition of the Trade Unions and the threats of those S.A. leaders who had wanted nationalisation of industry, great industrialists like Gustav Krupp were able to handle huge profitable orders. The money they had paid into Nazi funds reaped rich dividends.

THE YOUNG PEOPLE

If Hitler's dream of a Nazi empire lasting a thousand years were to come true, then the youth of Germany had to be converted into fanatical believers of Nazism. Older people whether Catholic or Communist might resist him, but Hitler knew they would eventually die off. Then only the young Nazis would be left. As usual Hitler acted quickly.

In June 1933 Germany's youth associations were taken over by the Nazis and placed under the control of Baldur von Schirach. From the age of six to eighteen boys served in various organisations in which they practised camping and sports and were 'indoctrinated' with Nazi ideas. The last four years were spent in the Hitler Youth where great stress was laid on indoctrination and preparation for military service. Girls served in the League of German Maidens working on farms and in factories, but Hitler did not regard them as being as important to the Nazi State as the boys. The girls were encouraged to marry and have large families (the future Nazi armies).

By 1938 there were nearly seven-and-three-quarter million members of these Youth Organisations but nearly half that number of young people stayed outside, in spite of severe penalties for parents who refused to co-operate. The most

The League of German maidens passing the Brandenburg Gate

promising boys were sent to 'Adolf Hitler' schools where they were specially trained to become the future Nazi leaders.

The control of education was of course of the highest importance to Hitler's plans. All professors, lecturers and teachers had to be believers in Nazism or they were dismissed. Textbooks were rewritten to fit in with Nazi ideas (especially history). The standard history textbook was called *Der Weg zum Reich*—'The Way to the Reich'. It was 250 pages long and dealt with all German history from the beginnings to Hitler. Nearly 2,000 years of history was covered but a quarter of the book was devoted to the eleven years of Nazism! There were no deliberate lies in the book but many important things were left out and great stress was laid on the 'enemies of the Empire'—the French and the Jews. It was strictly forbidden to teach religion. There were even great bonfires made of 'anti-Nazi' books in Berlin and other big cities.

Storm-troopers burning 'anti-German' books

THE ARMY

Of all the organisations in Germany only the army was in a position to halt the Nazis during the early part of Hitler's rule. Realising that he must first win the support of, and later control over, the army, Hitler treated the generals with the greatest respect and care.

The massacre of Ernst Röhm and his friends in 1934 was largely a move to please the army, which regarded the S.A. as an impudent rival. Also pleasing to the army were Hitler's promises to increase the size of the armed forces and eventually to 'expand' (by military attack) into eastern Europe. The army believed it could control Hitler, allow the Nazi promises to be kept, and then replace them as rulers. But by the time some officers decided the Nazis should be stopped it was too late. Hitler's grip had become unbreakable.

Hitler had secured his first hold over the army when he became President in 1934, and every soldier had been forced to swear an oath of personal loyalty to him. During the next four years the generals were kept busy and out of politics by the rearmament programme. In any case it was difficult for them to get near Hitler because he was so heavily guarded. Only General von Blomberg, the Minister of War, was close to

Hitler, but he was more a Nazi than an officer. By 1938 Hitler had gained the upper hand—Nazi ideas were becoming popular amongst army officers. Then a bombshell struck. The Commander-in-Chief of the army, General von Fritsch, was 'framed' by the secret police and forced to resign. The German officer corps stood by and scarcely lifted a finger to save him. At the same time von Blomberg, now a Field-Marshal, made a disastrous marriage and had to resign his post of Minister of Defence.

Hitler reorganised the command of the armed forces, giving himself even greater control. At one swoop he had shown that even generals could not stand in his path. The army had become a weapon of Nazism.

GENERAL, THAT TANK[1]

General, that tank of yours is some car.
It can wreck a forest, crush a hundred men.
But it has one failing:
It needs a driver.

General, you've got a good bomber here.
It can fly faster than the wind, carry more
    than an elephant can.
But it has one failing:
It needs a mechanic.

General, a man is a useful creature.
He can fly, and he can kill.
But he has one failing:
He can think.

The Instruments of Nazism

THE S.S. (SCHUTZSTAFFELN—PROTECTION UNITS)

The massacre of 30 June 1934 took place mainly in the Stadelheim Prison, Munich, and at the Lichterfelde Cadet School, Berlin. It was both the death-knell of the S.A. and the heralding to power of their executioners the S.S., the black-shirted guards of Nazism.

[1] Bertolt Brecht, 1938 (translated from the German by Christopher Middleton).

The two most feared men in Germany—Himmler and Heydrich

Formed in 1925 as Hitler's personal bodyguard, the S.S. grew into a vast and varied organisation. As the armed branch of the Nazi Party, under the command of Heinrich Himmler, it was to carry out by ruthless force the plans which Hitler had conceived for Germany and Europe. Most of the horrors which occurred in occupied Europe between 1933 and 1945 were the work of one or other section of the S.S.

Recruitment from the vast pool of unemployed was not difficult but standards were high. The S.S. were to be the supermen of the Third Reich; they had to be physically strong and intelligent and of 'Aryan' stock. Discipline was severe, training long and thorough, but above all blind obedience and loyalty to Hitler were the hallmarks of the S.S. trooper.

Walter Schellenburg, who joined the S.S. at the age of twenty-two and rose to be the head of the German Secret Service, explained why he chose the S.S.:

'All young men who joined the party had to join one of its formations as well. The S.S. was already considered an élite organisation. The black uniform of the Führer's special guard was dashing and elegant and quite a few of my fellow students had joined. In the S.S. one found the better type of people and membership of it brought considerable prestige and social advantage while the beer-hall rowdies of the S.A. were beyond the pale. In those days they represented the most extreme, violent and fanatical elements of the Nazi movement.'

TOTENKOPFVERBÄNDE (DEATH'S-HEAD UNITS)

Toughest of all the Nazis were men in charge of concentration camps and later the mass extermination camps (see page 157). Wearing the highly appropriate skull-and-crossbones badge, these companies were recruited on a twelve-year engagement. Many were convicted criminals who were released for this purpose. During their eleven years of operation the S.S. Death's-Head Units reached the lowest depths of murderous brutality ever witnessed by man.

In 1945 Allied officers who questioned captured S.S. guards came to the conclusion that most of these men had no idea of right or wrong. They seemed to carry no sense of guilt for the massive crimes they had committed.

Hitler's butchers—the SS

SICHERHEITSDIENST (S.D.-S.S. SECURITY SERVICE)
GEHEIME STAATSPOLIZEI (GESTAPO—SECRET STATE
POLICE)

These two services, although having different starting points, became increasingly similar in function. They were eventually brought under the control of S.S. General Reinhardt Heydrich ('the Hangman').[1] The main task of the S.D. and the Gestapo was to hunt down anyone who was critical of or hostile to the rule of the Nazis. With thousands of snoopers and informers penetrating into every factory, shop, office and school no man who valued his freedom, indeed his life, risked making even the slightest anti-Nazi remark. More than anything the success of this network strangled opposition to Nazism, for what man (there *were* some) was going to risk a sudden visit from the Gestapo by an unwise speech or action? Every man is basically afraid—how much more so when faced by the terror which the Nazi police units inspired.

When the war broke out the S.D. and Gestapo (founded in Prussia by Göring as a private 'gang') had the task of rooting out resistance leaders and partisan fighters in the occupied countries such as France. Most frightful of these activities were the systematic massacres of Jews and Communist officials in eastern Europe by the S.D. '*Einsatzgruppen*', sometimes assisted by local militia or other German units.

WAFFEN S.S.

The Waffen S.S. was the heavily armed branch which fought alongside the German army in France and Russia. It grew rapidly during the War from three to thirty-five divisions and had in its ranks men from many nations embodying Hitler's idea of a united Europe. It was to be a super-army and was expected to hold important positions. When the 6th S.S. Panzer Army was unable to stop the Russians outside Vienna in 1945 Hitler angrily ordered them to surrender their decorations and swastika-armbands. This they did—in a chamber pot!

THE POLICE FORCES

The local state police were quickly brought under Nazi control and the top positions were often given to S.S. officers. In 1936

---

[1] Killed by a bomb, thrown by resistance men, near Prague in 1942.

Himmler became police chief of all Germany and as chief of the S.S. as well he controlled an immense organisation. This meant that the local policemen would not interfere in the activities of, or investigate crimes reported against, the Nazis. This reduced the German people to a still more helpless position.

One of the massive Nazi party rallies at Nuremburg

THE LAW COURTS

The 'Enabling Law' had given Hitler power to make his own laws and with all police and S.S. units under his control they were rigidly enforced. For publicity purposes great trials were staged, but Hitler had no intention of letting his victims escape through Law Courts which might consider there was insufficient evidence for a conviction. Thus early in 1933 all magistrates and judges who were not Nazis were dismissed and successful defence lawyers risked beatings or imprisonment. When three Communists were acquitted at the Reichstag Fire Trial (1934) Hitler founded a new People's Court to deal with political (anti-Nazi) offenders.

Justice and the rule of law disappeared. Convicted Nazis often had their sentences quashed by the personal intervention of Hitler or another top Nazi. For an 'enemy' of the Nazis a verdict of 'guilty' was the normal foregone conclusion. Sometimes the judges were independent—but the Gestapo were waiting to whisk off the acquitted man to a concentration camp.

CONCENTRATION CAMPS

Soon after Hitler's appointment as Chancellor on 30 January 1933, prison camps began to appear all over Germany, staffed by the S.A. brownshirts but after 1934 by the S.S. The real or suspected enemies of the Nazis were seized and imprisoned without trial for varying periods suffering beatings-up, starvation, hard labour and even death. They included large numbers of Jews, Communists, Socialists, Catholic and Protestant clergy, gipsies, Freemasons, Jehovah's Witnesses or anyone who had been unwise enough to speak out against the Nazis.

One of the first to be arrested was Stephan Lorant, a Hungarian. He had become editor of the *Munich Illustrated Press* in 1925 and was taken into 'protective custody' on 12 March 1933. He was charged with Communist activity. Imagine Lorant's feelings as he walked down the prison corridor with the warder. He had had no trial, he had no idea how long he would be imprisoned or what his fate would be.

'You are being placed in solitary confinement.'

'For what reason?'

'Orders.'

'He unlocked the door of a cell. I was in cell number 40. Six paces long, two paces wide. There was no mattress as in number 47. There was only a wooden pallet and a sack filled with straw. At the foot of the pallet stood a water closet. The cell was cold and dismal, the radiator was out of order. . . . I lay down on the straw sack huddled up, shivering and freezing. Desperate, helpless, with no redress.'

78

Lorant was one of the fortunate ones. He was released after six months and immediately left Germany to live in England.

Wealthy people, including the hated Jews, could secure better treatment, even save their lives and gain their freedom, provided they were prepared to pay highly enough. (S.A. and S.S. men who accepted bribes were acting directly against Hitler's orders.) But fear of the Nazi police and a 'visit' to one of the concentration camps at Dachau, Buchenwald or Sachsenhausen was soon sufficient to drive opposition deeply underground. It stilled protesting voices to a whisper during the twelve years of Nazi rule.

PROPAGANDA

Newspapers and books. All Germany's newspapers were eventually brought under Nazi control and were forced to support their ideas and actions. Jews of course were banned from newspaper work and any editor who refused to join the Nazi party was dismissed.

Many newspapers such as the *Berliner Tageblatt* went out of business, but many others survived as long as they printed what the Nazis wanted. The Nazis had several of their own magazines and papers, the main one being *Völkischer Beobachter*, but the strangled press became very dull and sales dropped.

All authors had to be approved by the Nazis and no book could be published without their permission. As already mentioned a large number of books of both living and dead writers were burned publicly by young storm-troopers if it was thought these books had anti-Nazi ideas in them.

The best-seller in Germany at this time was Hitler's *Mein Kampf*. While few were prepared to plough through several hundred pages of very dull writing, it was considered 'safe' in most households to have a copy prominently on view. The sales of the book were so vast that Hitler must have come close to being a millionaire.

Films. All German-made films preached Nazi ideas whether they were comedies, thrillers, or romance. The result was that most people became heartily sick of such dull fare and tended to visit cinemas showing foreign films.

Radio. The age of mass-broadcasting by radio had scarcely be-

Dr Joseph Goebbels, Hitler's most loyal follower

gun when the Nazis came to power but it was to prove a most effective way of guiding the thoughts and minds of the German people. Hitler's speeches and those of other Nazis repeated over and over again the same basic ideas—expansion eastwards, hatred of the Jews—until many people came to believe in them, just as many people eventually believe repeated advertisements. The radio could be switched off but listening to foreign stations during the war, especially the BBC, was made punishable by death.

Here is a typical extract from an anti-Communist broadcast in 1937. It was entitled 'At first they were Seven'—referring to the No. 7 Party card held by Hitler.

A female voice: When you have been through the days of horror of the Munich Soviet Republic—
Second voice: and the atrocity of the Spanish civil war—
First voice: and the abominable suffering of the Russian nation itself—

80

Second voice:	when you have seen all these horrors, this poverty, this frightful blood sacrifice of Communist terror all over the world—
First voice:	then you come to the end of your journey in a room that shows pictures of the Third Reich—
Second voice:	and the frightful nightmare lifts—as if you came out of a dark cellar again into the bright light and the sun—
First voice:	and then you go on and remain standing for a while in front of a picture of the Führer—

All the methods of mass-communication mentioned above were harnessed by Dr Goebbels to preach Nazism to the German people. In the early years they told of the glories and successes of Nazism and until 1943 the great victories of the *Wehrmacht* (army). In the last months of the War the people were urged on to greater efforts by warnings of the terrible vengeance which would fall upon them at the hands of the Allied forces.

Since it was impossible, or at least highly dangerous, to hear the 'other side' of the story, massive propaganda became one of the Nazis' most successful weapons.

3 Hitler on the Road to War: 1933—39

Hitler's Plans for Europe

Some European statesmen who had never read *Mein Kampf* believed that Hitler merely wished to tear up the Versailles Treaty and return Europe to its condition of 1914, before World War I. Hitler had far more sweeping plans than this, based upon the twin principles of the Germanic unity and German living space.

German unity meant the gathering together of all Germans in Europe, one people into one empire, ruled by one leader. This involved people living in Austria, Czechoslovakia, Danzig, Memel and in other isolated pockets. Germany had not enough farmland to feed her population or enough raw materials to supply her factories. New lands to the east—in Poland and Russia—would therefore have to be taken over. These territories were, of course, to be made 'Jew-free'.

Hitler intended to destroy the power of France for ever but he hoped to take Great Britain into partnership after settling the question of the former German colonies. He also regarded Rumania highly because of her oil wells, and respected Yugoslavia because of her fine army. His overall vision was of an alliance of eastern European states, dominated by Germany, to form a buffer against the Russians and 'Asiatics'. Hitler valued the friendship of Italy, but in 1933 had not become an ally of Mussolini. For some time therefore the two dictators regarded each other warily.

European Reactions

The Russians knew what Hitler's intentions were and reacted swiftly. Since 1917 Russia had been excluded from Europe. The refoundation of the Polish state at Versailles had been conceived partly as a barrier to keep Communism out of Europe. Now France brought Russia back into Europe.

Threatened in the east by Japan and in the west by Germany, Russia was only too happy to enter into agreements which might restrain her potential enemies. So in 1934 she became a strong supporter of the League of Nations, which formerly Russians had described as a 'robber band of capitalist states'. The next year she signed a defensive pact with France and Czechoslovakia. Russia had become a new problem for Hitler.

Poland was in a difficult position because she now occupied former German lands. Previously she had been France's leading friend in eastern Europe. France was now drawing closer to her (Poland's) former enemy, Russia, so that the Poles turned to Hitler and in January 1934, hopefully signed a ten-year pact with Germany. It was to survive less than six years.

France was thoroughly alarmed by Hitler's seizure of power and hastened to complete the Maginot Line fortifications. It was hoped that this great wall would keep the Germans out. France's fear played a major part in undermining the World Disarmament Conference of 1932–34. Deeply suspicious of Germany, she was quite unwilling to agree to the MacDonald plan which called for the reduction of all armies. Meanwhile she sought to encircle Germany by the alliance with Russia and smaller European powers. Time was to show how worthless these treaties were.

Britain, secure behind the Channel, treated the threat of Nazism much more casually. Sir Horace Rumbold, British Ambassador to Berlin from 1928 to 1933, wrote a private letter in 1932 in which he compared Hitler to a 'revivalist preacher with the appearance of a greengrocer, wearing an Air Force moustache'. In 1935 Lord Lothian visited Hitler and wrote afterwards: 'I am convinced Hitler does not want war'. G. Ward-Price thought Hitler was a 'human, pleasant personality' with a 'strong strain of sadness and tenderness in his disposition'.

Not everyone agreed with these assessments of Hitler. Winston Churchill asked, 'What manner of man is this grim figure who has . . . loosed these frightful evils?' Professor Stephen Roberts, an Australian who had stayed in Germany, said quite bluntly: 'Hitlerism cannot achieve its aims without war . . . the German people are ready to accept war.'

83

In 1933 when Hitler came to power the horrible memory of World War I was still so strong that many in Britain were prepared to go to almost any lengths to avoid war. War was the only way in which Hitler could be stopped and with both the U.S.A. and Britain unwilling, attacking Germany was a ridiculous idea. If Hitler were overthrown Germany would return to the terrible chaos of 1923. In any case nobody believed Germany could become a real threat for ten years. This was true but as A. J. P. Taylor has commented, 'they failed to allow for the fact that Hitler was a gambler who would play for high stakes with inadequate resources'.

As Hitler's actions and demands became more menacing during the next five years western European statesmen retreated and gave way in the hope that Hitler would be satisfied. This policy of 'appeasement' was to fail because there were no limits to Hitler's ambitions. Many people now believe that a really determined stand against Hitler in 1934 or 1935 would have blocked his trail of conquest for ever. When it was obvious that appeasement had failed it proved too late to stop Hitler without a long and terrible struggle.

The First Steps

After less than a year in office Hitler withdrew Germany from the League of Nations, and followed this by a pact with Poland. Later in 1934 Hitler suffered his first set-back when an attempt by Austrian Nazis failed to overthrow the government in Vienna. Mussolini brought troops to the southern frontier of Austria as a warning to Hitler not to interfere. The Austrian Chancellor, Engelbert Dollfuss, was mortally wounded by Nazis and allowed to bleed to death on the floor of his study. Doctor Kurt von Schuschnigg then took over as Chancellor until 1938, 'protected' by Mussolini.

Following Mussolini's action, Britain, France and Italy formed the Stresa front to prevent the destruction by individual countries of the Treaties which might endanger world peace. In order to secure the participation of Italy, France had to make certain concessions in Africa. This gave Mussolini the impression that the French would not interfere if he decided to press his claims in Abyssinia.

In 1935 Hitler had further successes. The important coal-mining area of the Saar voted by ten to one to return to Germany. In March Hitler felt confident enough to announce that he was abandoning the Treaty of Versailles by introducing conscription to bring the army up to 500,000 men. He was further able to split the Western Allies by concluding a naval treaty with Britain by which Germany was allowed a surface fleet equal to 35 per cent of the Royal Navy and also a submarine fleet. Britain was influenced to a large extent by France's independent attitude. Accepting that German rearmament was 'here to stay', the British leaders decided that the best solution was to come to an agreement with Hitler. Mussolini, who now seemed closer to France than to Germany, invaded Abyssinia in October. Attempts by the Allies to hold up or to stop the invasion failed and by May 1936 the conquest was complete. The League of Nations proved helpless and Hitler knew he could act without fear of the consequences.

The Rhineland, 1936

By the Treaty of Versailles Germany was forbidden to station troops or build fortifications within thirty miles of the Rhine. In the event of war, France would enjoy a big advantage over Germany, and to Hitler this state of affairs was intolerable. The French-Russian alliance signed on 27 February 1936 gave him the final proof and on 7 March small forces of German troops crossed the Rhine bridges and entered the 'forbidden'

German troops cross the Rhine at Cologne, 1936

zone. The French army, which far outnumbered the Germans, made no move to stop them. Had they done so the Germans had orders to retreat quickly. In Britain the majority feeling was that Hitler had every right to occupy his own country.

More Successes, 1936

In July civil war broke out in Spain. The Republican Government, supported by the Socialists and Communists, was attacked by the Nationalists led by General Franco. Hitler decided at once that he would help Franco in order to prolong the war as much as possible. This would distract France and draw Mussolini, who was becoming heavily involved in Spain, nearer to Germany. In fact by 21 October a secret agreement had been signed in which Germany and Italy would work together in foreign affairs. A month later Germany and Japan signed an anti-Communist Treaty, soon to be signed also by Italy.

It was still less than four years since Hitler had become Chancellor. He had moulded Germany into a proud, vigorous and united nation once more, with rapidly growing armed forces. He had, it seemed, found two powerful allies while shattering the unity of the Western powers. The time had now come to put his plans fully into action.

Austria, 1938

The 7 million German-speaking inhabitants of Austria—the land of Hitler's birth—were to be the first acquisition to the new German Empire. Having bungled in 1934 Hitler sent Franz von Papen as ambassador to Vienna in 1936, to work for the overthrow of von Schuschnigg. Von Papen recommended strong measures, and he got them. Austrian Nazis made bomb attacks on public buildings and organised huge parades throughout 1937. Finally on 12 February 1938 Hitler summoned von Schuschnigg to meet him at Berchtesgaden, the Führer's mountain residence. For two hours Hitler stormed, raved and threatened: 'The whole history of Austria is just one long act of treason to the German race', and later: 'Who knows perhaps you will find me one morning in Vienna like a spring storm. Then you will go through something! . . . The

S.A. and the legion will come in after the troops . . . wreaking vengeance.'

After lunch Ribbentrop, the German Foreign Secretary, presented von Schuschnigg with a draft of Hitler's demands. These included lifting the ban on the Austrian Nazi Party and the release of imprisoned Party members. Three Nazis were to be given seats in the Austrian Cabinet: Seyss-Inquart as Minister of the Interior, Glaise-Horstenau as Minister of War, and Fischbok as Minister of Finance. Finally, Austria was to be tied closely both economically and militarily to Germany. Von Schuschnigg tried to get the terms modified, but in vain. Hitler allowed him three days' grace before the Agreement came into force, and von Schuschnigg reluctantly signed. He then returned to Vienna and four days later began to carry out Hitler's demands. Hitler was well satisfied, for he realised that Austria was going to fall into his lap without any need for revolution. During the following weeks, the Austrian Nazis began to behave more and more boldly. It was obvious that before long they would be in complete control of the country. Von Schuschnigg then acted with blind and desperate courage. On 8 March he ordered a plebiscite to be held to decide whether Austria should remain independent or unite with Germany. This meant that every Austrian would vote and the result might destroy Hitler's argument that most Austrians wanted an *Anschluss* (union with Germany).

Hitler was furious at the news and ordered plans for a military invasion to be drawn up. They would be carried out only 'if other measures proved unsuccessful'. Meanwhile, a letter was sent to Mussolini to seek his support, for it was he who had largely prevented a German take-over in 1934. Later Hitler issued orders for the possible invasion of Austria—'Operation Otto'.

It was still hoped to gain control without an invasion. First the Nazis secured the abandonment of the plebiscite, and then the resignation of von Schuschnigg. When they tried to replace him by Seyss-Inquart, the President of Austria, Wilhelm Miklas, refused. In spite of threats from Berlin, Miklas stood firm, but as the day wore on, news of Nazi uprisings throughout the country poured in. At last Miklas yielded. Seyss-Inquart became Federal Chancellor of Austria, but Hitler re-

The German Army occupying Vienna, 1938

fused to stop the occupation of the country by German troops. He had already received news from Rome that Mussolini would not interfere.

Early on the morning of 12 March 1938 advance patrols of the German army crossed the frontier. In the afternoon Hitler himself drove through the streets of Linz, to an enthusiastic reception. He spent the night in the town, deciding there and then to incorporate Austria into the German Reich.

Soon, motorised units of the German Eighth Army were pouring over the passes and down the valleys of Austria. Many vehicles broke down on the way, which helped to delay Hitler's arrival in Vienna. Nevertheless, huge crowds turned out to greet him when he did arrive. Now just a quarter of a century since he had slipped out of the city unnoticed and unwanted, Hitler returned as lord and conqueror.

A month later a plebiscite was held to seek approval of his action. The vote was 99·75 per cent in favour. Speaking to a press conference, Hitler said: 'This is the proudest hour of my life'.

Behind Hitler came Himmler and the Gestapo. A special concentration camp was set up at Mathausen and the usual victims of Nazism, those who had been unable to escape or buy their freedom, became the first inmates. Hitler had increased

88

Hitler's triumphal return to Vienna after twenty-five years

his empire by 7 million and opened the road to his next conquest: Czechoslovakia.

Czechoslovakia, 1938–39

STAGE ONE

Czechoslovakia had come into existence in 1918 at the Treaty of Versailles. The population of 14 million was composed of the former inhabitants of Bohemia, Moravia and other smaller territories. The Czechs represented half the population and the Slovaks 2 million. Hitler's interest lay in the northern part, the Sudetenland where there were 3 million German-speaking inhabitants. Under the Presidency of Thomas Masaryk (1918–1935) and Eduard Beneš (1935–39), Czechoslovakia became a free country surrounded by Nazi, Fascist and Communist dictatorships.

Hitler had long hated the Czechs—they were 'subhuman' in his eyes, a free people and allies of his deadly enemies, France and Russia. Their fine army had to be destroyed before he could move east and by seizing Austria he was now able to outflank the northern defences. In addition Czechoslovakia was cut off from her allies, so help was not likely to come. But the greatest danger to the Czechs came from within—the 3 million Sudeten Germans. They had been inspired by the

Anschluss (union with Austria) and they too wanted to join the great German Reich.

Konrad Henlein, the physical education teacher, who led the Sudetenlanders, said in 1936: 'As Germans in the Sudeten provinces . . . we feel ourselves members of the great cultural community of Germans in the whole world.'

Hitler did not, therefore, create the Czech crisis—he merely took advantage of it. He had no intention of making a head-on attack upon Czechoslovakia but intended to increase tension and conspire and threaten until somebody's nerve broke.

The leading statesmen of Europe evidently believed that Hitler only wanted 'justice' for the Sudeten Germans. Once again they hoped that by satisfying his immediate appetite he would not invade Czechoslovakia and plunge Europe into war. The French Government was so divided on the question of whether they should support Czechoslovakia that they sent a message to Britain, begging Chamberlain to make the best bargain he could with Hitler. It was for this purpose that the seventy-year-old British Prime Minister, Neville Chamberlain, was to make three flights to Germany in September 1938 to talk to Hitler. Chamberlain sought only to avoid war. In a broadcast to the nation before leaving he said: 'How horrible, fantastic, incredible that we should be digging trenches . . . here because of a quarrel in a far away country between people of whom we know nothing.'

Chamberlain sent a telegram to Hitler on the 13th suggesting that he should set off for Germany the next day. Hitler was delighted, but to conceal his feelings, he casually awaited Chamberlain's arrival in the Berghof, a seven-hour plane journey from London. On a stormy afternoon the two leaders sat down to discuss the fate of several million Czechs. As could be expected, Hitler talked and Chamberlain listened, but it was a rambling monologue with hints of war, and Chamberlain began to feel that his journey had been wasted. Finally, Hitler agreed to the peaceful detachment of the Sudentenland areas following a plebiscite. Secretly he continued preparations for an invasion.

During the following week, Chamberlain sought the agreement of the French and the Czechs to the terms which he and Hitler had arrived at. Meanwhile pressure on Czechoslovakia was increased by demands from Poland for Teschen, from Hungary for Moldavia, and by the Slovak people's party for self-rule. If these three demands in addition to Hitler's were met, it would mean the complete break-up of Czechoslovakia.

Chamberlain arriving for the Munich Conference

On 22 September Chamberlain again flew to Germany and met Hitler at Godesberg on the Rhine, and reported that he had secured the consent of the British, French and Czech Governments. Hitler replied: 'I am exceedingly sorry but after the events of the last few days this solution is no longer any use.' Chamberlain was angry and puzzled. He failed to realize that Hitler's real objective was the destruction of Czechoslovakia by force. The demand for the Sudetenland was merely an excuse to invade. Finally a compromise was reached. The Czechs would evacuate the Sudetenland by 1 October. 'This', said Hitler, 'is my last territorial demand in Europe.'

But the British Cabinet refused to yield to Hitler's demands. A promise of support was sent to France if she became involved in war with Germany over Czechoslovakia. Chamberlain continued his lone quest for peace and tried to persuade Hitler not to attack President Beneš in a forthcoming speech. Sir Horace Wilson, Chamberlain's special envoy, met Hitler but had to submit to a storm of interruption and insults as he presented his case. Finally, Hitler invited Wilson and the British Ambassador to the Sportspalast to hear him speak—a speech which turned out to be a long, vicious attack against Czechoslovakia and its President. The clouds of war gathered darkly.

Chamberlain then sent a message to Mussolini asking him for support in the plan which he was addressing to Hitler: an international conference to give Hitler what he wanted. Hitler telephoned Mussolini and agreed to hold a meeting at Frankfurt or Munich provided Mussolini came in person. Mussolini agreed on Munich and invitations went to Daladier and Chamberlain.

The Munich meeting was held in the newly built Führerhaus, with the delegates seated in easy chairs round the room. The discussions were repeatedly interrupted and often broke into heated arguments. Eventually terms were agreed, and the dictators left the two Western leaders with the task of informing Beneš of the dismemberment of his country. Beneš resigned the presidency.

On 1 October German forces entered the Sudetenland. On the 10th Poland took Teschen, and three weeks later Hungary's claims were satisfied. Hitler and Chamberlain signed a pledge 'never to go to war with each other' and everyone was happy. Everyone, that is, except Czechoslovakia which, with no representative at Munich, eventually lost one-third of her territories and population to Germany and Hungary.

Chamberlain was greeted as a hero in London. 'Come straight to Buckingham Palace', said King George VI, 'so that I can express to you personally my most heartfelt congratulations'; and *The Times* applauded: 'No conqueror returning from a victory on a battlefield has come home adorned with nobler laurels.'

More delegates at Munich, *L. to R.* Göring, Ciano, Hitler and Mussolini

Oi! who's the fat wanker

STAGE TWO

The tiger had been fed but he was still ravenous. Throughout
the winter of 1938–39 the Nazis made plans for the final destruction of the Czechoslovak State. Hitler's reasons were
mainly economic ones. The seizure of the great Škoda armament works and the gold and foreign currency reserves in
Prague would be an immense relief from the strain of German
rearmament. German newspapers began to fill with stories of
violence by the Czechs upon Germans in that country.

'GERMAN BLOOD FLOWS AGAIN IN BRUNN.'

'HUMILIATION OF GERMAN HONOUR.'

'GERMAN STUDENT BEATEN UP.'

To protect these 'unfortunates' Hitler began to mass troops on
the frontier and on 15 March 1939, in an effort to save his
country, President Hacha (who had succeeded Beneš) took a
train for Berlin. He was kept waiting until 1 a.m. before being
admitted to the presence of Hitler, Göring and five others.
After an attempt to curry favour with Hitler, Hacha was forced
to listen to a long speech, which ended with Hitler telling him
that the German army was going to invade Czechoslovakia at
6 a.m.—in less than four hours' time. Göring then warned

93

The result of Munich. German troops enter the Sudetenland, October 1938

Hacha that if the Czech army resisted, Prague, the capital, would be bombed. Hacha fainted, but after being revived put through a telephone call to his government telling them not to resist. He then signed an agreement asking the Führer to 'protect' his people.

Within four days the German garrisons were in complete occupation and the new members of the puppet government in control. The British and French ambassadors could only mumble inadequate protests.

Clouds of War, 1939

Hitler's seizure of Czechoslovakia was his first aggressive move against non-Germans. Even Chamberlain realised that Hitler could no longer be appeased and said so on 17 March.

Exactly two weeks later Britain gave a solemn promise of help in the event of attack to Hitler's next obvious victim— Poland.

Hitler then cancelled his 1934 'No war' treaty with Poland and his 1935 naval agreement with Britain, and followed this by a ten-year military alliance with Italy. Far away across the Atlantic the U.S.A. regarded the squabblings in Europe as none of her business. Another giant, Russia, regarded everyone with suspicion and could not be left out of the reckoning.

The Poles had good reason to fear Nazi Germany. Lands which they had acquired from Germany in 1919 cut off East Prussia from the Reich by the Polish Corridor and separated Danzig from Germany in order to give Poland a seaport. For a time Hitler remained friendly towards Poland, hoping to form an alliance with her against Russia. When Hitler started demanding the return of Danzig the Poles realised that German friendship would be of little value. These fears were further confirmed when German troops occupied Czechoslovakia on 15 March 1939 and then moved into Memel a week later. Only worry about the attitude of Soviet Russia held up Hitler's march into Poland, so the Germans began to drop hints that they would like to become more friendly with Russia. But neither side would make a move.

German annexations, 1938–39

The French and most Englishmen could see that it was no use promising to help Poland without Russia's support. An alliance with Russia was repugnant to a great many Englishmen. In a letter to his sister in 1939 Neville Chamberlain wrote: 'I must confess to the most profound distrust of Russia.

I have no belief whatever in her ability to maintain an effective offensive even if she wanted to. And I distrust her motives. . . .' A neutral Russia, however, would be able to control Europe if Germany, Britain and France fought to the death. In the event of a Russo-German war the winner would also be in a controlling position, so Britain adopted the impossible policy of trying to keep at peace with Germany by an alliance with Russia.

Negotiations in the summer of 1939 between the British and Russians came to nothing because the former wanted to warn Hitler against attacking Poland, while the latter wanted a military alliance which could defeat Germany. This belief of the Russians that the Western Allies wanted her to fight Germany alone led to the bombshell of 22 August 1939—the Russo-German non-aggression pact.

By this Russia and Germany agreed not to go to war for twenty-five years. The door was left wide open for Hitler to move into Poland.

The Polish Agony

It only remained for a shallow excuse to be provided for the invasion of Poland. A series of incidents were faked on the frontier, the most famous being at Gleiwitz, organised by Alfred Naujocks, a Gestapo officer. Twelve German criminals dressed in Polish uniforms were killed and left lying near a German radio station. Shots were fired, a broadcast made and members of the Press invited to see the 'evidence' of the wicked 'Polish' attack.

Nine hours later at dawn on 1 September 1939 Hitler's forces set out to 'punish' the Poles. Great columns of tanks, mobile guns and lorries poured over the frontier while overhead the dive-bombers screamed in for the kill.

Two days later, on the refusal of Hitler to withdraw his forces, first Britain then France declared war on Germany. But this belated action could not save Poland. In spite of the utmost bravery the Poles found that cavalry regiments were no match for tanks. Their air force was destroyed on the ground. Their commanders were captured and mobile German units sprang from nowhere to prevent retreat and mop up resistance.

The Russians were surprised by the speed of the German

advance and moved in hastily to claim their share of Poland under the August Agreement. Meanwhile the last units of the Polish army were being rounded up and on 30 September, after a desperate siege, Warsaw surrendered.

The faces of these Polish children illustrate the terrible suffering of civilian populations during the War

Yes! there boys will do.

Walter Schellenburg, a young S.S. officer, walked through the ruins. 'I was shocked at what had become of the beautiful city I had known—ruined and burnt out houses, starving and grieving people. A pall of dust and smoke hung over the city and everywhere there was the sweetish smell of burnt flesh. . . . Warsaw was a dead city.'

The horror of war had again descended upon Europe.

97

Summary of the Causes of World War II

1 'Hitler's dictatorship was devised to wage war.'[1] Nazism sought unlimited power through trickery, threats and violence. From the moment Hitler came to power, Europe began sliding towards war. Less than nine months after his seizing power, Germany left the Geneva Disarmament Conference and the League of Nations. In 1934 and 1935 Hitler sought to isolate France by making paper promises to Poland and England. Also in 1935 he scrapped the Treaty of Versailles and began rearming. Dr Schacht was appointed 'to direct all economic preparation for actual war'.[2] In 1936 Hitler boldly tested French and British resolution by retaking the Rhineland. By 1938 the German rearmament programme was well under way, with expenditure that year reaching £1,710 million. This was more than twice that of Britain and France put together. By 1938 Hitler had also gained complete control of the army, and knew that he could act without fear. The occupation of Austria, the Sudetenland and Czechoslovakia followed in quick succession. By the spring of 1939 the Allies realised that only war could stop Hitler conquering all Europe.

2 'This is not a peace. It is an armistice for twenty-one years.'[3] The Treaty of Versailles made the majority of Germans very bitter. They were able to delude themselves that payment of reparations was the cause of their misery. Hitler used the bitter memories of Versailles to gain support for himself. Versailles left Germany angry but unbroken, which explains the truth of Marshal Foch's prophecy.

3 The economic depression (1929–31) destroyed the newly-found prosperity of Germany and helped to sweep Hitler into power. It also destroyed much of the spirit of friendship which was developing amongst European nations.

4 Some of the responsibility for smoothing Hitler's path must rest with other great powers.

Japan, Germany's 'double' in the Far East, began undermining the League of Nations in 1931, when she occupied Manchuria, and continued the process in 1937 with an inva-

[1] David Thomson, *Cambridge Modern History*, vol. 12, C.U.P.
[2] Arthur Schweitzer, *Big Business in the Third Reich*,
[3] Marshal Foch in 1919.

sion of China. Nearer to Europe, Mussolini's Italian forces gained a quick victory in Abyssinia (1935–36). The League of Nations stood by helplessly as troops, weapons and money from Italy, Germany and Russia were poured into the blood-bath of the Spanish Civil War.

By 1939 it was obvious that the League of Nations was a distant memory. All the pacts, treaties and promises made during the previous twenty years had collapsed like a house of cards.

The role of the Western powers during this period is not a proud memory. The U.S.A. had withdrawn from Europe almost immediately after Versailles. The knowledge that the world's greatest power was a silent spectator gave Hitler great comfort. France was almost paralysed by fear of another German invasion. Although weaving a web of alliances with Poland, Czechoslovakia and Russia, she was not prepared to take any action unless actually attacked by Germany. Great Britain comes out of it little better. Failing completely to understand 'the lengths of evil, dishonesty and deception to which the Nazi mentality could extend'[1] the British leaders, apart from Churchill, believed that Hitler's demands could be satisfied. Not until the breaking of the Munich agreement did Britain take a firm stand and solemnly warn Hitler. By then Germany had become strong enough to laugh at the warnings of the 'stuffed lion'.

Finally, Russia—the great outcast. Stalin had not ignored Hitler's speeches attacking Communism, but he knew in 1939 that Russia was not ready for war. Deeply suspicious of the Western Powers, he was quite ready to sacrifice Poland in order to buy time. Stalin's diplomatic somersault, the signing of the 1939 Nazi-Soviet Pact, was the match which ignited the European powder-barrel.

Greedy, suspicious, frightened or over-confident though Europe's leaders might have been, it was still Hitler who actually started the war by his violent attack on Poland in September 1939. He had probably not contemplated having to take on Britain, Russia and the U.S.A. all at once: never has history provided a better example that 'he who lives by the sword shall die by the sword'.

[1] Sir J. W. Wheeler-Bennett, *Munich: Prologue to Tragedy.*

4 Hitler at War: 1939—45

The 'Phoney War'

With the defeat of Poland the world sat back to await the next
move. By this time Britain had only 150,000 troops in Europe
and the French showed no signs of leaving the shelter of the
Maginot Line. The next move had therefore to come from
Hitler. He was keen to invade France at once but on the
advice of his generals waited until the spring of 1940. An
American journalist called this period of waiting the 'Phoney
War'.

Before we go on to see what happened when Hitler went to
war against the Great Powers—France, Britain, Russia and
America—let us see what methods of fighting were used.

How the War was Fought

THE BACKGROUND

In 1935 Hitler said: 'If I were going to attack an opponent
. . . I should suddenly, like a flash of lightning in the night,
hurl myself upon the enemy.'

While armies do not move at the speed of lightning, World
War II was remarkable for the immense distances covered at
speed by the opposing forces. These movements were made
possible only by the development of the internal combustion
engine fitted into aeroplanes, tanks and lorries. This meant
that oil was of the greatest importance to all the nations taking
part. World War I (1914–18) had been fought almost at a
standstill. Huge masses of men had hurled themselves at
barbed wire and machine-guns and had been slaughtered by
the thousand every day. The horrible memory of this war had
made men like Chamberlain vow there must never be another.
Hitler and certain generals like Heinz Guderian realised that
dive-bombers and tanks could succeed in breaking through
where the infantry masses had failed. A colonel, Charles de

Gaulle, was a lone voice in the French army protesting against the Maginot Line, an immensely expensive defence network stretching from Switzerland to Belgium but not to the Channel coast. The cost of the Maginot Line meant that France was short of modern tanks and aeroplanes.

The economic problems of the 1930s had led to great cuts in defence spending in both Britain and the U.S.A. Russia had spent more but in 1939 was still some way behind Germany in the quantity and quality of her equipment.

Thus when war broke out Germany had the strongest army and air force in the world and was building a navy which was to cause considerable trouble, especially with its submarines, to the Allies.

THE BLITZKRIEG

Warfare of rapid movement and ruthless attack, pioneered in Germany, became known to the world as the 'blitzkrieg'. It required surprise—Hitler never bothered to declare war—force and boldness. To achieve success there was complete co-operation between tanks, artillery and infantry and between ground forces and air forces.

The 'blitzkrieg' usually began shortly before dawn. Dive-bombers of the Luftwaffe (air force) attacked the enemy air force on the ground, anti-aircraft batteries, army barracks and headquarters, bridges and railway centres. Thus in a few hours the enemy was unable to strike back in the air or bring up its heavy equipment and reinforcements by rail. Units which tried to move by road were also attacked.

Two or three hours after the dive-bombers, the panzer (tank) divisions moved into action. The usual attack was in the form of a gigantic pincer movement which surrounded the enemy and cut off his retreat. Motorised infantry, following up, dealt with the trapped troops while the panzers continued their deep penetrations. Sometimes the panzers moved so fast that they captured enemy generals and headquarters. This deprived the army of its 'brain' without which it could not fight properly.

The German army was also the first to use paratroops to capture bridges, strong-points, and airfields. These were of great value to the advancing army and air force. Since paratroops cannot be heavily armed, they suffer heavy losses if met by strong opposition. This happened to both the British (Arnhem, 1944) and the Germans (Crete, 1941). Britain developed 'commando' units to raid or demolish enemy head-quarters, radar stations, bridges and airfields. But perhaps the most amazing exploit of this type was carried out by an S.S. squad under Otto Skorzeny. In 1943 Benito Mussolini, the Italian dictator and ally of Hitler, had been overthrown. He was imprisoned in a mountain-top hotel which could be reached only by a railway. Skorzeny and his men landed by glider on the mountain-top, rescued Mussolini without a drop of blood being spilt, and took off from a rock-strewn meadow in a Fieseler-Storch aeroplane.

STRATEGIC BOMBING

In 1919 an Italian general, Giulio Douhet, wrote: 'Take the centre of a large city and imagine what would happen among the civilian population during a single attack by a single bombing unit. . . . What could happen to a single city . . . could happen to fifty cities . . . normal life would be impossible in this constant nightmare of imminent death and destruction. . . . [There would be] a complete breakdown . . . in a country subjected to this merciless pounding from the air.'

Britain and the U.S.A. adopted Douhet's idea with enthu-siasm and built up strategic bombing forces to put it into prac-tice. As the U.S.A. did not enter the war until 1941 it fell to Britain to try to win the war by the lavish use of heavy bomb-ers. Neither Germany nor Russia saw any point in destroying what they hoped to plunder. Moreover the Luftwaffe did not start to bomb London and other British cities until the R.A.F. had already made several raids over Berlin and the Ruhr. The Luftwaffe had been built to increase the hitting power of the army—it was in fact a force of flying artillery. Britain on the other hand was to devote nearly half of her whole war effort to the construction of heavy bombers with the result that the army and navy were desperately short of vital equipment such as landing-craft.

THE FAILURE OF THE BOMBER

Almost from the start of the war Britain began dropping bombs on Germany. The first aim was to destroy all German

A four-engined Lancaster bomber being loaded with an 8,000 lb. 'block-buster'

industry by what was called 'precision' bombing. These raids took place at night so very often the target was missed altogether; dummy targets and specially lighted fires fooled many bomb-aimers and meanwhile the growing strength of the German anti-aircraft batteries and fighter planes took heavy toll of the cumbersome bombers. By 1943 250 bombers a month were being built, yet losses of men and machines over Germany were so great that R.A.F. Bomber Command was unable to expand. In spite of the repeated attentions of the R.A.F. and the U.S.A.A.F. German factories increased their total production of war materials, between January 1942 and September 1944, by over 300 per cent!

DESTRUCTION OF THE CITIES

In 1942 the Allied Air Chiefs decided, perhaps on aerial photographic evidence, that 'precision' bombing was not enough. It was, therefore, decided to try to destroy German fighting spirit by what Douhet had called 'a merciless pounding from the air'.

On the night of 30 May, the first 1,000-bomber raid took place on Cologne.

From 24 to 31 July, Hamburg was raided eight times; 80,000 civilians were killed and 60 per cent of the city destroyed mainly by incendiary (fire) bombs. Elsa Wendel, a housewife, described the horror of that week.

'A great flame was shooting straight out towards them. A flame as high as the houses and nearly as wide as the whole street. As she stared in fascination the giant flame jerked back and then shot forward towards them again.'

'My God, what is it?' she said.

'It's a fire-storm,' the old man answered.

'The beginning of one. Quick, come along, there's no time to lose. . . . We must run.'

Hamburg after a R.A.F. bombing raid

The strategic bombing forces were diverted from the German cities to assist the Allied invasion of Europe in 1944. Here the bombing of railways, roads, bridges and oil refineries proved of great value to the war effort. Once the invasion was assured the lure of the cities was too great and the bombers crowded over their now rubble-heap targets so closely that they were almost colliding. During the last quarter of the war when German defeat was certain no less than four-fifths of all the bombs used in the war were dropped.

The climax came on the night of 13 February 1945, by which time the German armies were being crushed to pieces in East and West. The city of Dresden, swollen to a population of over 300,000 by refugees, was the chosen target. Although the advancing Russians were only fifty miles away it was deemed necessary to despatch in relays nearly 3,000 British and American bombers over the defenceless city. The result can be left to your imagination.

The result of this destruction in the words of Major-General Fuller was that 'while the First (Russian) and Second (Anglo-American) Fronts were advancing to win the war the Third Front (The Bombers) was engaged in blowing the bottom out of the peace which was to follow its winning; for cities and not rubble-heaps are the foundations of civilisation.'

THE WAR AT SEA

Submarines. On the day Britain declared war on Germany, the liner *Athenia* carrying 1,400 passengers was torpedoed in the Atlantic. This attack, by submarine *U-30*, although directly against Hitler's orders, set the scene for what was to follow.

In less than three months German U-boat commanders had been given permission to sink all hostile ships, on sight and without warning. However, this U-boat fleet was in its infancy so that in the first months of the war there were rarely more than six in the Atlantic at any one time. From the beginning of the war Britain adopted the convoy system, protection at first being limited to an armed merchant cruiser. As the ship-building programme developed, corvettes, frigates and destroyers equipped with radar and asdic devices took over the protection of convoys. Special aeroplanes were also designed to 'hunt' and 'kill' submarines.

These protective measures took nearly four years to become fully effective. By 1941 the number of operational U-boats had rise to sixty. Operating from bases in occupied France, they hunted in packs, spreading out to search for prey, closing in once it had been found. Heinz Schaeffer, commander of U-boat *U-977*, described a 'kill'.

'We attack again. It's easy now for we are just over a thousand metres away. They've spotted our periscope, though, and with their machine-guns and quick firers let fly at us, endangering the periscope glass. We attack from another quarter and dive under the ship at ten fathoms. The hydrophone operator reports "She's right overhead".

'This time we're going to use the stern tube which we don't often get the chance to use. "Range four hundred metres . . . fire!" The roar's terrific. We've fired from much closer this time; under water the noise is frightful. The tanker has broken in two.'

By 1942 the situation was critical for Britain. Cargo vessels were being sunk at the rate of nearly twenty a week but fortunately anti-submarine measures were rapidly improving. By the end of the war nearly 800 U-boats had been sunk out of a total of 1,162. The German, Italian and Japanese forces had destroyed a total of 5,150 allied merchant vessels.

On the surface. By 1939 the age of massed fleet battles had gone.

German U-Boats. This picture was taken at the end of the war when they were being handed over to the Royal Navy

Hitler realised he could not challenge Britain's naval strength, so he had built few large warships. The Italian navy fared badly against the British Mediterranean fleet and Hitler failed to capture the French fleet when he conquered France.

Lack of sea power was a severe handicap for Germany. It meant that the projected invasion of England (1940) remained only a dream while the Allies could carry out theirs of North Africa (1942) and Normandy (1944) with complete success. It enabled Britain to evacuate over 300,000 men from Dunkirk (1940) by sea but spelled disaster for almost a similar number of Germans and Italians trapped in Tunisia (1943).

Probably the most famous incident was the sinking of the German battleship *Bismarck* on 27 May 1941. Crippled by torpedo attacks from planes and destroyers, the *Bismarck* was finally finished off by the British battleships *King George VI* and *Rodney*.

The Campaign in North-West Europe, 1940

NORWAY AND DENMARK—APRIL

Before turning on his main enemies in the West, Britain and France, Hitler first decided to secure his northern flank. In conquering Norway and Denmark he intended to secure three objectives.

1 A long coastline from which his U-boats and raiders (disguised warships used for attacking merchant ships) could operate. This would force the Royal Navy to divert large forces to the North Sea.

2 To stand astride the sea route between Britain and Russia.

3 To protect his supply of iron ore from Sweden. This was vital for the building of tanks and guns.

Denmark collapsed with scarcely a shot being fired, since resistance would have been useless against overwhelming German forces. The country was taken by surprise and when the people of Copenhagen saw German soldiers marching towards the Royal Palace they thought a film was being made!

Norway proved more troublesome but though there was some spirited resistance the result was never in doubt. The Norwegian Nazi Party under Vidkun Quisling persuaded many important people that occupation by Germany would be a good thing. The German invasion itself was a masterpiece of skill and deception. Merchant vessels filled with German troops entered the main harbours of Norway and over-whelmed the local defences. Norwegian Nazis, aided by German paratroops, seized the main airfields. The main German forces, seven divisions in all, were then landed and resistance quickly destroyed.

German victory. Allied troops were landed at ports in the north but they were too weak to throw out the Germans. Lacking air cover their position was hopeless and after a fortnight they were evacuated by the Royal Navy.

German success was due to the boldness and speed of the attack. Norwegian fighting power was stunned before it could retaliate. The reputation of the German armed forces was greatly increased whilst in Britain the failure of the Allies to stop the Germans brought the downfall of Neville Chamberlain's government. On 10 May 1940 Winston Churchill became Prime Minister and remained so until July 1945.

FRANCE AND THE LOW COUNTRIES

(Belgium, Netherlands and Luxembourg)

The line-up. Hitler was still determined to conquer Russia but he dared not attack eastwards while his rear was menaced by the British and French. He therefore had to secure his western front and accordingly by November 1939 had assembled 140 divisions, including 10 panzers, opposite the 120 of the Western Allies.[1]

Although almost equal in numbers the Allies were much weaker in equipment and there was scarcely any co-operation amongst the four Allied armies. The largest of the four, the French, were sitting timidly behind the Maginot Line with no idea how the Belgians and Dutch intended to fight. It was these two armies which were defending the gap between the end of the Maginot Line and the sea.

The collapse of Holland and Belgium. At midnight on 9 May Hitler struck. Bombers roared over Dutch airfields, destroying her air force and attacking important headquarters. Paratroops

---

[1] There were about 18,000 men in an infantry division; a panzer division had fewer men and about 250 tanks.

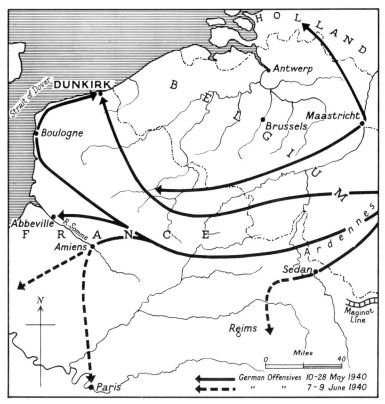

The conquest of N.W. Europe

captured airfields, bridges and other important strong-points. Rotterdam was heavily bombed and within six days Dutch resistance collapsed.

Belgium suffered a similar fate although it was not until the eighteenth day of fighting that King Leopold ordered the Belgian army to surrender. Meanwhile the situation in France had become critical, mainly due to outdated thinking on the part of the Allied commanders.

The German breakthrough. The original German plan had been for the panzers to sweep through Holland and Belgium, as had been tried in 1914. General von Manstein, who proved to be Hitler's most brilliant commander of the war, argued against this. He suggested the main attack should come through the centre, through the hilly wooded country of the Ardennes. The

French, believing this area to be impossible for tanks, were defending it with their weakest forces.

The attack began on 14 May and succeeded beyond all belief. General von Kleist's panzers tore a forty-mile gap through the Allied line. By the 17th they had reached Amiens, on the 20th Abbeville, on the 23rd Calais. With their backs to the Channel, nearly 400,000 French and British found themselves hemmed in on all sides by the German forces. Capture seemed inevitable—then the 'miracle' took place.

German troops resting in a French village, June 1940

German jigolos discussing their latest lays.

DUNKIRK

On 24 May the Allies had only one port left open—Dunkirk—and in answer to a BBC broadcast hundreds of boats from the south and east coasts converged on it. During the next week over 330,000 troops were 'lifted' off the beaches and brought to safety in England.

A British officer described the scene on the waterfront at

Dunkirk: 'Along the promenade, in parties of fifty, the remnants of practically all the last regiments were wearily trudging along. There was no singing and very little talk. Everyone was far too exhausted to waste breath! Occasionally out of the darkness came a sudden shout: "A Company, Green Howards . . ." "C Company, East Yorks . . .'.

'These shouts came either from stragglers trying to find lost units or guides on the lookout for the parties they were to lead onto the Mole for evacuation. The tide was out. Over the wide stretch of sand could be dimly discerned little oblong masses of soldiers moving in platoons and orderly groups down towards the edge of the sea. Now and again you would hear a shout: "Alf, where are you?" "Let's hear from you, Bill." "Over this way, George."'

The reasons for the 'miracle'. The failure of the German army to force the surrender of the Allies at Dunkirk was probably the result of a number of circumstances and decisions. When Hitler ordered his panzers to halt on 23 May the idea of evacuation by sea never entered his head. The Allies were trapped and would wait. In any case his panzers were urgently in need of servicing and refitting. With about 40 per cent already out of action there was a strong possibility of more heavy losses amongst the dykes and canals around Dunkirk. The main thrust over the Somme to Paris would then have been seriously delayed. No doubt Göring was keen to secure some of the glory from the generals by allowing the Luftwaffe to 'mop up' the Dunkirk pocket. At any rate Hitler's order to halt was long enough (forty-eight hours) to allow the defence of the beachhead to be strengthened and the evacuation to take place. Although the evacuation was a magnificent achievement, it should be realised that Dunkirk was a resounding defeat for Britain.

THE COLLAPSE OF FRANCE: JUNE 1940

On 5 June the Germans crossed the Somme, and on the 14th entered Paris. Meanwhile the French government had retreated to Bordeaux and on the 17th requested an armistice (cease-fire). Mussolini joined the war on Hitler's side on 11 June and was present at the signing of the armistice on 25 June. Until 1942 the Germans occupied only the northern half

A French woman staring at the ruins of her home

Fido! Fido! Where are you.

of France. The remainder was ruled by the French Vichy government, closely supervised by the Germans.

THE FORTY DAYS

In less than six weeks Hitler had achieved what the Kaiser's army had failed to do in four years (1914–18). German dead numbered 'only' 27,000, less than half the number of British casualties in one day in 1916. The German attack had mainly sought to avoid destruction. The Luftwaffe had dive-bombed enemy units and reinforcements but not factories or roads. Speed and surprise were once again the key factors, backed by superb organisation. Engineers travelled with the leading panzers to clear minefields and rubble, bridge rivers and repair damaged vehicles. The Luftwaffe answered the calls from the ground forces to attack strong opposition while in some cases the R.A.F. was away bombing the Ruhr.

THE BATTLE OF BRITAIN

Hitler's next logical step was to plan an invasion and conquest of Britain. It has always been believed that if the R.A.F. had been destroyed by the Luftwaffe, the German army would have been free to cross the Channel and complete its mission. Hitler's plan in fact was doomed before it even started.

With the destruction of the R.A.F. it was felt that the Royal Navy would be 'neutralised'. Certain German admirals and air force generals were by no means certain that the Royal Navy could be prevented from breaking up the invasion fleet, even by the massed ranks of the Luftwaffe. Even if the invasion fleet could be assured safe passage where were the assault boats coming from? Germany had very few, nor was the army trained in amphibious (sea and land) operations. Rough seas or a thick fog would endanger the whole operation and the problems of further supply would be considerable. Eventually the objections of the German Navy became so persistent that Z-day (date of invasion) was postponed three times. Finally on 12 October 1940 the whole project was 'shelved' and Hitler began to prepare for an even bigger adventure.

In July when the project was still considered possible, Göring began laying his plans for the destruction of the R.A.F. Probing attacks were made on Channel convoys and south coast towns, but early in August the 'Battle of Britain' really got under way. Between 13 August and 7 September the Luftwaffe made an all-out attack on the R.A.F. but failed to achieve the planned destruction. Much of the battle was taken up with 'dogfights' between British Spitfires and Hurricanes and German Messerschmitts. Wing Commander Johnny Johnson took part in many such encounters. 'Throughout it all the radio is never silent—shouts, oaths, exhortations and terse commands. You single out an opponent. Jockey for position. All clear behind. The bullets from your eight guns go pumping into his belly. He begins to smoke.'

Then on 8 September when the R.A.F. was nearing exhaustion the Luftwaffe suddenly switched its attacks to bombing raids on London. It was hoped to paralyse the government and cause a stampede out of the tortured capital. For a week the attack continued, by which time the R.A.F. had recovered sufficiently to smash up the largest attack yet launched, 1,300 planes. From this point on the German attack was doomed— by the end of October they had lost over 1,700 planes. Nevertheless the bombing of London and other important cities continued throughout the winter. The success of the R.A.F.

was mainly due to the highly effective warning system based on radar and the Observer Corps. The information received was passed on to operations rooms which in turn alerted the fighter stations. The oncoming Luftwaffe were intercepted each time, by whatever strength the R.A.F. could muster. Instead of being widely scattered the fighters could concentrate where they were most effective. In addition Fighter Command, increasingly equipped with the faster Spitfire, had been specially trained in defensive fighting.

AMERICAN AID

During this testing time for Britain, American help began to arrive. Although the U.S.A. was neutral a system of 'cash and carry' was developed which enabled Britain to collect war materials from her ports. Germany could also have done so but she was prevented by the strength of the Royal Navy. This strength was increased in the autumn of 1940 by the exchange of fifty American destroyers, to assist in convoy work, in return for bases in the West Indies. Finally in January 1941 President Roosevelt instituted 'Lend-Lease', by which the U.S. government was empowered to dispose of war materials to help in the defence of the U.S.A. This meant in fact sending the equipment to Britain.

War with Russia, 1941-44

WHY HITLER TOOK THE PLUNGE

Even before the Battle of Britain had begun Hitler ordered the OKW—the High Command of the Armed Forces—to begin planning for the invasion of Russia in 1941. Hitler did not believe that an unconquered Britain would be a threat. He thought Russia would collapse as quickly as France and Poland had, after which Britain would call for peace.

Hitler was sure that the Russian forces would be quickly destroyed, remembering defeats by Japan (1904) and Germany (1917), and her poor showing against the tiny Finnish army (1939); the mass trials of thousands of Russian army officers in 1938 leaving her very short of experienced leaders; and finally the brilliant achievements of the German army in 1939-40. These were the facts that Hitler bore in mind, when he said confidently to General Jodl: 'We have only to kick in the door and the whole rotten structure will come crashing down.'

The conquest of Russia was Hitler's most important aim. With such a vast addition of land and wealth, Germany would soon become equal in power to the U.S.A.; eventually master of the world—or so Hitler thought.

Since 1939 Stalin, the Russian dictator, had been sending all kinds of vital supplies, such as oil, to Germany. He hoped these would buy off Hitler but the latter wanted *all* Russia's wealth. This meant occupation by German troops, which the Russians would resist. So on 18 December 1940 Hitler issued 'Operation Barbarossa'—the order for the invasion of Russia on 15 May 1941.

Preparations were proceeding smoothly when suddenly Hitler's attention was diverted to the south-east, a diversion which William L. Shirer has called 'the most catastrophic single decision in Hitler's career'.

WAR IN THE BALKANS

In April 1939 Mussolini had attacked and conquered Albania and in October 1940 he tried to add Greece to his Empire. A fierce battle at Tepeleni in March 1941 destroyed Mussolini's hopes, but more worrying to Hitler had been the arrival of 57,000 Allied troops in southern Greece.

Soon afterwards Hitler persuaded Yugoslavia to sign an alliance with him, but two days later there was an anti-German revolution in Belgrade. In fury Hitler unleashed his armies on Yugoslavia and Greece, postponing the invasion of Russia for five weeks. On 6 April Belgrade was heavily bombed and the Allied forces were driven relentlessly back. First Yugoslavia then Greece were conquered but fortunately for the Allies three-quarters of the British forces, comprising Australian, New Zealand, Polish and English forces, managed to escape by sea.

Once again the superior air power and armour of the Germans won the day. The Allied position was hopeless from the start but they had promised help to Greece and the promise had to be kept.

Crete. The German campaign was completed by the successful invasion of Crete. This was the first time a complete army was carried, landed and supplied from the air. On 20–21 May

The conquest of the Balkans, 1941

thousands of paratroops and glider troops landed. Although seaborne landings were completely smashed, the Allied troops were overwhelmed. Between 28 May and 1 June 14,500 men were rescued by the Royal Navy out of the original garrison of 27,000.

The attack on Crete was one of the boldest and most superbly organised of the war. German ground and air forces acted as one whereas the British had little air support. There were no aircraft carriers in the vicinity and the nearest R.A.F. units had to be called up via Cairo from the Western Desert.

THE ATTACK ON RUSSIA, JUNE 1941

Hitler's aims. Hitler launched his attack on Russia exactly three weeks after the last British troops left Crete. He hoped to destroy her armies before Britain could recover or the U.S.A. decided to enter the war. Before the winter set in he hoped to have his troops along a line Leningrad–Moscow–Volga (see

Operation Barbarossa—The attack on Russia

map No. 6). Realising that conquest of the whole U.S.S.R.—one-sixth of the world's land surface—was impossible, he planned to go only as far as the Ural Mountains. Here he would establish a defence line to keep the 'asiatic hordes' out of Europe. The Russian people were to be driven into Siberia or allowed to starve to death. Their places would be taken by German settlers protected by S.S. garrisons.

The plan of attack. The German forces were directed in three great spearheads; a total of over 3 million men equipped with nearly 10,000 tanks and 3,000 aircraft.

1 Army Group North, commanded by Field-Marshal von Leeb, consisted of two armies and one armoured group. Its target was to capture Leningrad and cut the railways to the Arctic ports from which Allied help might come.

2 Army Group Centre, commanded by Field-Marshal von Bock, was the largest of the spearheads. The three armies and two powerful panzer groups were ordered to capture Moscow. Not only was Moscow the seat of government and an important industrial centre but it was the hub of Russia's railways. Its capture would paralyse troop movements from the east.

3 Army Group South, commanded by Field-Marshal von Rundstedt, was ordered to occupy the Ukraine, the centre of Russian wheat-growing. From there he was to press on to the coal-mining area of Donetz and then capture the Caucasian oilfields. For these tasks he was given three armies and one armoured group including a large force of Rumanians.

Progress of the attack. The fierce German attack in the early hours of 22 June evidently took the Russians completely by surprise. The blitzkrieg seemed to exceed even Hitler's wildest hopes. Army Group North reached Riga on 30 June, Narva on 20 August, and laid siege to Leningrad on 8 September. Army Group Centre reached Minsk on 10 July, and on the 16th, after advancing 450 miles in three weeks, attacked Smolensk. A fierce battle lasted until 7 August, but such were the German losses they were not able to resume the advance until 2 October. Army Group South crossed the Russian frontier on 5 July and reached Kremenchug on 1 September. This was followed by a tremendous encirclement of 700,000 Russian troops at Kiev at the end of September. Rostov was taken on 21 November, but recaptured by the Russians a few days later.

German difficulties. It was not surprising that by the autumn of 1941 the world believed that the conquest of the Soviet Union was only a matter of time. The German forces had advanced hundreds of miles and had taken a fantastic number of prisoners. One German soldier, Benno Zeiser, wrote of his meeting with some of these men.

Some of the three million Russian soldiers captured by the Germans in 1941

'We suddenly saw a broad, earth-brown crocodile slowly shuffling down the road towards us. From it came a subdued hum, like that of a beehive. Prisoners of war. Russian, six deep. We couldn't see the end of the column. As they drew near the terrible stench which met us made us quite sick; it was like the biting stench of the lion house and the filthy odour of the monkey house at the same time. But these were not animals, these were men.'

These men had not surrendered easily. Even when sur-rounded the Russians fought with a determination and bravery which shocked the Germans and caused them heavy losses. In spite of this great number of prisoners the main Russian armies had escaped. The Germans had stuck to the roads and tracks but the Russians melted into the forests and became partisans. As the war progressed the partisan raids and attacks became increasingly troublesome. Perhaps the greatest tech-nical difficulty came with the railways. The Russian broad-gauge lines were useless for German locomotives and rolling stock. Engineers had to follow the advancing armies relaying every yard of line. All weapons, ammunition, food and cloth-ing had to be brought along these lines as the Russians had re-moved or destroyed almost everything of value.

The advance on Moscow. After the two-month delay at Smolensk, Hitler ordered an immediate attack on Moscow before winter came. Two huge pincers advanced quickly through Gomel-Orel-Tula to the south and Smolensk-Vyazma-Rzhev to the north. But as Moscow came nearer so the advance slowed down. The winter came early and as the snow fell the tracks became thick with mud. The wheeled supply vehicles were un-able to move—the advance slithered to a halt. Then the temperature dropped sharply, the mud froze and the advance resumed. The temperature continued to drop. The Germans lacked winter clothing and thousands of cases of frostbite were recorded although Heinrich Haape found it possible to get warm clothing from the Russians! 'The bodies were frozen stiff. And those invaluable boots were frozen to the Russians' legs. "Saw the legs off", ordered Kageneck. The men hacked off the dead men's legs below the knee and put the legs, with boots still attached, into the ovens. Within ten or fifteen min-utes the legs were sufficiently thawed for the soldiers to strip off the vital boots.'

As well as men, vehicles and locomotives were affected. Petrol froze and the men had to light fires under vehicles to start them. The Russians were conditioned to the cold and brought up thousands of tough, fresh and warmly-clad Siberians to the front—the 'winter army'.

The Russians hit back. By early December scouting parties of 258th infantry division had reached the outskirts of Moscow,

The first terrible Russian winter caught the Germans unprepared

Ok! who came all over the Moscow

but had to be pulled back. Then with the temperature −40°C, General Zhukov, Russia's leading soldier, struck out. A hundred divisions attacked all along the Moscow front smashing through the German lines. A panic retreat, like Napoleon's in 1812, seemed likely but Hitler ordered 'no retreat'. After a seventy-mile retreat the line held in spite of heavy losses and the Germans retreated into vast fortified camps called 'hedgehogs'. Russian ski-troops swarmed around but could not break in.

Many generals who had disobeyed the 'no retreat' had been sacked and Hitler had taken complete command, but worse news had already descended on Germany. The day after General Zhukov's counter-attack, Japanese warplanes attacked the American fleet at Pearl Harbour. Hitler hastily declared war on the U.S.A., expecting Japan to do the same on Russia, but he was mistaken. As his armies retreated for the first time over the bleak, frozen steppes, Hitler must have reflected that whereas six months ago he had had only Britain to worry about now he was at war with the world's three greatest powers.

THE ROAD TO DISASTER, 1942-43

German position. When the snows began to melt Hitler took stock of his position. His armies were still deep in Russia but the cost had been enormous. The casualties—killed, wounded and captured—amounted to 35 per cent, or over 1,100,000 men. Only 10 per cent of his panzers were ready for action and supplies and equipment had been rapidly used up in the 'hedgehogs'.

During the spring General Keitel, Göring and finally Hitler himself went cap-in-hand round the satellite states begging for extra troops. When the campaign opened they had secured 27 Rumanian divisions, 13 Hungarian, 9 Italian, 2 Slovak and 1 Spanish, but all were below German standards in training, equipment and fighting spirit. These weaknesses were to help to bring disaster down upon the Germans.

Even Hitler realised a mass advance on the lines of 1941 was impossible. Instead of destroying the Russians he decided to wear them down by destroying their communications (railways) and depriving them of oil.

German plan for 1942. The main effort was to fall on Army Group South and it was heavily reinforced. Most oil for the Russian armies came up the Volga from Baku. Therefore, Hitler reasoned, if he captured Stalingrad oil supplies could be cut off. Unfortunately, Hitler was too greedy and wanted to capture the oilfields for his own use. In July the 4th Panzer Army, which could have walked into Stalingrad, was diverted south for the thrust on the oilfields. To cover these southerly attacks a defensive position Kharkov–Voronezh–Saratov–Stalingrad was to be established—from Saratov Moscow could be attacked in the rear. Strong resistance at Voronezh led Hitler to order General von Hoth's 6th Army to turn south-east to Stalingrad instead of east to Saratov.

This put the Germans into a highly dangerous position as their main forces were now in two long almost unprotected arrow-head formations. Hitler had left them wide open to a smashing counter-attack.

The Battle of Stalingrad. In August 1942 the 6th Army and 4th Panzer Army penetrated into Stalingrad, a long straggling industrial city. The German bombs and shells soon turned the city into a rubble-heap and for over five months thousands of

The German advance in Southern Russia, 1942

men fought the most savage battle of the war over this prize. At the beginning of this book we met Sergeant Pavlov, who held his house in Stalingrad for nine weeks in spite of fierce German counter-attacks. Throughout the whole long struggle both sides fought with amazing courage, determination and often brutality in spite of immense losses.

The death of an army. The long exposed flanks of the 6th Army worried Hitler's generals, even more so when reports came in of huge Russian build-ups in front of these flanks. General

Halder suggested a retreat from Stalingrad, but Hitler roared, 'Where the German soldier sets foot, there he remains.'

Nobody, except perhaps Hitler, was greatly surprised when at dawn on 19 November 1942 three huge Russian attacks burst through the flanks. These flanks were guarded mainly by unwilling Hungarians, Italians and Rumanians. In five days the Russians had completely surrounded the twenty-two divisions, about 250,000 men, in Stalingrad. The Russians had expected a retreat but Hitler ordered the 6th Army to 'hedgehog'. This meant they would have to be supplied by air— 750 tons a day. This would need a transport plane to land in Stalingrad day and night once every six minutes. As this was impossible Hitler gave permission for a relief force to break through. The Russians drove this back at Christmas, sealing the fate of the encircled Germans.

The Russians offered to allow the 6th Army to surrender but Hitler forbade it. Russian loudspeakers tried to persuade individual Germans to give up—one record repeated over and over again was: 'Every seven seconds a German soldier dies— Stalingrad—Mass grave.'

The 6th Army was dying as the Russians tightened the net around it. Benno Zeiser who had witnessed the plight of beaten Russians now describes the beaten Germans:

'Completely cut off, the men in field grey slouched on, invariably filthy and invariably louse-ridden, their weary shoulders sagging from one defence position to another. The icy winds of those great white wastes which stretched for ever beyond us to the east lashed a million crystals of razor-like snow into their unshaven faces, skin now loose-stretched over bone so utter was the exhaustion, so utter the starvation. It burned the skin to crumpled leather. It lashed tears from the sunken eyes which from over-fatigue could scarce be kept open, it penetrated through all uniforms and rags to the very marrow of our bones.'

On 31 January Field-Marshal Friedrich von Paulus and the remnants of his Army, 93,000 men, surrendered to the Russians.

In the meantime the German forces in the Caucasus had beaten a skilful retreat to Rostov. But nothing could disguise the fact that Hitler's order to 'stand fast' had resulted in the greatest defeat Germany had yet suffered. The Russians now began to move forward—to Berlin.

THE RUSSIAN STEAM-ROLLER

By March 1943 the Russian attack came to a halt. Then in July the Germans launched their last massive attack on the Russian front. Half a million men including seventeen panzer divisions hurled themselves on the Russians at Kursk. After a week the attack petered out and the Russians went on to the offensive. The Germans fell back at the rate of two or three miles a day selling every inch of ground dearly. Russian tactics were to attack at one point to exhaustion, halt, then immediately reopen the attack on another sector. This gave no rest to the Germans who were now outnumbered three to one in men and nearly five to one in tanks and guns.

In January 1944 Leningrad, which had been under siege for 900 days, was relieved. The Finnish army was defeated in June and dropped out of the war in September. In July the German Army Group North was cut off by the Russians while to the south Marshal Rokossovsky approached Warsaw. 'On 28 June 1944, 6th Division was encircled near Bobruisk. At their backs flowed the river of Napoleon's final defeat—the Beresina. And on the other bank, between 6th Division and their homeland, stood the Russians. The last order was given: "Redundant weapons to be destroyed; only iron rations and ammunition to be carried. Code word 'Napoleon'—every man for himself." The men of the Infantry Regiment 18, every man of the proud 6th Division fought like devils. Little Becker fell, so did Oberfeldarzt Schulze. Major Höke fought and died at the head of his regiment; heavily wounded, he saved his last bullet for himself. A few crossed the river and slipped through the Russian trap; most died on the banks of the Beresina; a small remnant was captured and marched away into captivity. Perhaps a hundred men, not many more, struggled through the Pripet Marshes and reached their homeland—a hundred from the eighteen thousand men who had marched into Russia under the Bielefeld crest. 6th Division, the heroic Regiment 18, had ceased to exist.'[1] Rumania was overrun at the end of August 1944, causing the loss of valuable oil to the Germans.

[1] H. Haape, *Moscow Tram Stop*.

5*

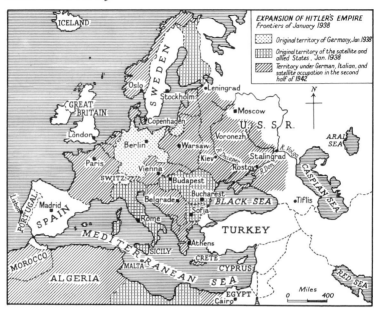

Hitler's Empire at its greatest extent

As the winter of 1944–45 approached the Russian armies prepared for the final assault upon Germany; through East Prussia and Warsaw to the north and through Budapest, Vienna and Prague to the south.

The Mediterranean Campaigns, 1940–44

THE POSITION IN 1940

Hitler had agreed with Mussolini that the Mediterranean should become an 'Italian lake'. This meant the British must be pushed out of Egypt and out of their smaller bases in Cyprus, Malta and Gibraltar. Three months after entering the war Mussolini urged his North African army to march on Egypt. The Italian 10th Army in Libya numbered some 215,000 men and in addition there was an equal number stationed in East Africa. Opposing this mighty force were some 55,000 British and Indian troops.

THE FIRST ALLIED VICTORY

The Italians advanced sixty miles and then proceeded to build a series of badly-sited and poorly-defended forts. General

Wavell, therefore, decided to take the offensive instead of waiting. On 9 December the 7th Armoured and 1st Indian Division attacked the forts and in two days captured 38,000 prisoners. The advance was resumed in January leading to the capture of Tobruk on the 3rd. The 7th Armoured Division then turned inland and cut off the retreat of the remaining Italians at Beda Forum. This brought the grand total of prisoners to 130,000.

Once again swift, daring attacks had proved superior to stationary defence. The three services worked as a team— the navy bringing up supplies and the air forces bombing Italian forces. Fortunately the Italians were not keen to fight so the task of the British was made much easier.

THE ARRIVAL OF ROMMEL

Worried by Italian defeats Hitler dispatched German forces— the Afrika Korps under General Rommel—to shore up Mussolini's forces. At the same time General Wavell had to dispatch forces to Greece (see page 115). Rommel hit hard and soon regained the 500 miles which the Italians had lost, but he was too late. If Hitler had sent troops four months before he would have destroyed British power by cutting her off from the East and seizing the oilfields of the Middle East. Instead he was juggling with the hopeless problem of invading Britain.

STRUGGLE IN THE DESERT

For well over a year Rommel sought to break through to Egypt. The 'Desert Fox', as he was known, was a brilliant commander who personally controlled his forces in battle. He kept his forces concentrated and could swing them at a moment's notice when he detected a weakness. In the summer of 1942 he destroyed the British defence positions. Then he recaptured Tobruk, taking 30,000 prisoners, and reached the Egyptian frontier and El Alamein.

Unfortunately for Rommel he was weakened by loss of supplies in the Mediterranean. Sometimes as many as 75 per cent of his cargo vessels were sunk. Neither could he persuade Hitler to take much interest in North Africa. The Führer was becoming increasingly tied up with the Russian front and regarded North Africa as a sideshow.

British Soldiers examining a wrecked German Tank in Libya

In August 1942 Rommel made his last desperate attack to break through the 8th Army positions, now under the command of General B. L. Montgomery. After drawing the panzers onto his anti-tank screen, Montgomery counter-attacked vigorously but halted his troops after three days. He was not ready yet for the main attack.

THE ROAD TO TUNIS

In October 1942 Rommel had 95,000 men and about 550 tanks facing Montgomery's strongly reinforced army of 150,000 men and 1,100 tanks. For once the German–Italian army, under the temporary command of General Stumme, was badly placed.

The Battle of El Alamein began with a fourteen-day air bombardment which destroyed the German–Italian air force. Then at 9.40 p.m. on 23 October 1,000 guns roared out along the forty-mile front and the long march to Tunis began. Lt. Weiner Schmidt caught the full impact of the Allied attack:

'Now a shiver went through me. From out of the dip emerged rank after rank of new tanks—a good sixty in all. They came at us with every muzzle blazing. I got my right gun into

128

action. It stopped one tank. Several others were burning but
the bulk of them came on relentlessly. What was wrong with
my left gun, I wondered. It was silent, its muzzle still drooping
to the ground. I leaped from the trench despite the stuff
whistling all round and raced to the gun.

'Two of the crew were sprawled on the ground. The
breech of the gun was shattered. The loader lay beside a wheel,
bleeding from a machine-gun bullet in the chest. "Water,
Water", he gasped.

'A fresh salvo burst beside the gun. Tanks were obviously
attacking it at point blank range. To stop there meant death.'

Rommel returned from Berlin and fought fiercely but within ten days the remnants of his armies were fleeing westwards
pursued by the victorious Allies.

ALLIED LANDINGS IN NORTH AFRICA

Meanwhile American and British forces under the command
of General Eisenhower had landed in Algeria on 8 November.
Threatened from the rear by this force and from the front by
the 8th Army which had travelled 1,400 miles in eighty-one
days, the Germans were heavily reinforced by the air force.
Hitler poured thousands of men into Tunisia to no avail. After
weeks of desperate fighting, the new commander, General von
Arnim, was forced to surrender on 12 May 1943 with 267,000
men. Allied warships patrolled the seas around Tunis to prevent a German 'Dunkirk'.

The Germans were defeated in North Africa because Hitler
failed to strike at the right moment. If Rommel had had at El
Alamein some of the thousands of troops who arrived in
Tunisia in 1943, he might well have burst through the 8th
Army to Cairo. Perhaps Hitler's biggest mistake was (once
again) to underestimate the importance of sea-power. It was
Britain's sea-power which enabled her to build up the power
of the 8th Army and complete the destruction of the Afrika
Korps.

THE COLLAPSE OF ITALY, 1943

Unconditional surrender. The two disasters of Stalingrad and
Tunisia in the first half of 1943 rang the death-knell of Nazi
Germany. Only a few fanatical Nazis, including Hitler him-

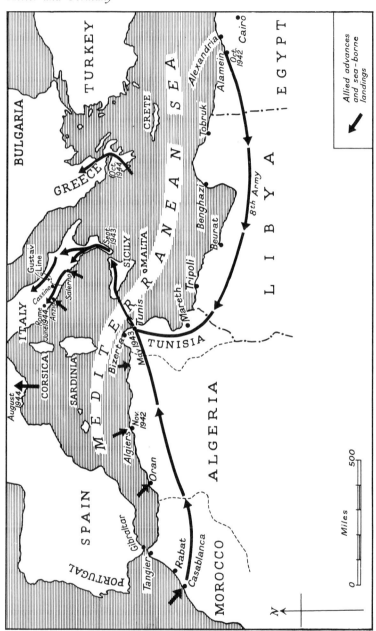

War in the Mediterranean Theatre, 1942–44

self, refused to believe that the war was lost. To save Germany
from utter defeat, and of course, thousands of lives, peace discussions should have begun.

Peace discussions were an impossible hope. In January 1943,
Churchill and Roosevelt had met at Casablanca and decided
on unconditional surrender by Germany. This meant surrender without any promises or guarantees. The Nazis used
this to urge the German people to greater efforts, warning
them of what would happen when the Allies took over Germany. Himmler was given even greater police powers to crush
the slightest sign of resistance. When the Allies later issued
lists of war criminals to be tried, and the Morgenthau plan to
strip Germany of all her industries, the Nazis became determined to fight to the death.

Invasions of Sicily and Italy. So the weary struggle went on. The
Allied commanders, having cleared up North Africa, decided
to invade Sicily and southern Italy. This would give control of
the Mediterranean, enable bombers to reach central Europe
and pin down German forces which could be used elsewhere.

The invasion of Sicily began on 10 July. It took the Allies
thirty-eight days to secure the island while the bulk of the
German forces escaped over to Italy. Allied sea-power enabled
the landing to be a complete surprise but the heavy bombers
failed to prevent the German retreat.

As the fourth year of the war began British troops landed on
Italian soil; five days later, the 5th Army landed at Salerno
and the slow, painful advance up the back of Italy began.

Mussolini overthrown, 1943. The invasion of Sicily sparked off a
revolt against Mussolini. On 25 July 1943 he was called to the
Royal Palace, dismissed by the King and placed under arrest.
He was then taken to prison in an ambulance.

Hitler was stunned by the news. Mussolini was his most
trusted ally and friend and had been an example to him
during his struggle for power before 1933. Guessing that the
new Italian prime minister Marshal Badoglio would seek to
make peace with the Allies, Hitler energetically began to prepare to take over power in Italy. To General Jodl he said:
'Work out the orders . . . telling them (the 3rd Panzer grena-
dier division) to drive into Rome with their assault guns . . .
to arrest the government, the king and the whole crew.'

131

The road to Rome. The armistice withdrawing Italy from the war was signed on 3 September and made public five days later—'a gigantic example of swinishness', Hitler called it. Instead of landing in the north of Italy and cutting off the Germans in the south, the Allies landed on the southern tip. They were then faced with the immense task of fighting their way up the mountainous back of Italy. Rivers, gullies, ravines

British Soldiers advancing through the ruins of Cassino

and mountain slopes all ran at right angles across the path of the Allied advance and had to be taken by storm. In December the Germans took their stand upon the River Garigliano. This position, known as the Gustav Line, included the mountain-top monastery of Monte Cassino. Believing it to be a German observation post the Allies rained bombs and shells upon it for three days. Even this was insufficient to remove the defenders, so the air forces turned to bombing roads and railways which carried German supplies.

In the meantime a seaborne landing had been made at Anzio in January 1944 with the aim of attacking the Gustav Line in the rear. Instead of attacking the Germans soon after landing the invading forces delayed. Bill Maudlin, an American war artist, described what happened when the Germans attacked:

'Anzio was unique.

'It was the only place in Europe which held an entire corps of infantry, a British division, all kinds of artillery and special units and maintained an immense supply and administration set-up without a rear echelon. As a matter of fact there wasn't any rear. There was no place on the entire beach where enemy shells couldn't seek you out. Sometimes it was worse at the front, sometimes worse at the harbour. Quartermasters buried their dead and amphibious truck drivers went down with their craft. Infantrymen dug into the Mussolini canal had the canal pushed in on top of them by armour piercing shells and Jerry bombers circled as they directed glider bombs into LST's and Liberty ships. Wounded men got oak leaf clusters on their purple hearts when shell fragments riddled them as they lay on hospital beds. Nurses died. Planes crash-landed on the single airstrips.'

Anzio held; the Gustav Line was stormed and the Germans retreated. On 4 June 1944 American forces entered Rome, the first European capital to be recaptured from the Germans. But two days later even worse news arrived in Hitler's headquarters.

A huge Anglo-American army had crossed the Channel and landed on the Normandy beaches. Western Europe was also going to be torn from Hitler's grasp.

The Collapse of Hitler's Empire, 1944-45

THE DECISION TO INVADE WESTERN EUROPE

Although some believed that Germany could be defeated by bombing alone, most of the Allied leaders came to realise that the German armies must be defeated on land. This meant an invasion; a second front which would also take pressure off the Russians.

Working on the Atlantic Wall. Hitler hoped to make Europe into an impregnable fortress

Nazis building sand castles

The question of when to invade was delicate for a failure would be costly and might eventually lead to a Russian conquest of Western Europe. A miniature invasion of Dieppe by 6,000 Allied troops—mainly Canadian—in August 1942 had been heavily defeated. Casualties had amounted to nearly 70 per cent, causing one officer to call it a 'seaborne charge of the light brigade'. Shortage of landing craft led to a postponement in 1943 so the summer of 1944 was fixed as the time to try.

Normandy was selected because it was close to Britain. The invading army, future reinforcements, and supply ships would not have far to travel. The sheltered beaches were ideal for the landing and were flanked by two excellent ports, Cherbourg and Le Havre. Finally by destroying bridges over the rivers Seine and Loire all German forces in Normandy would be cut off from help or retreat.

The size of the invasion forces was colossal. One-and-a-quarter million American troops had arrived to join a similar number of British. 4,000 landing-craft were assembled protected by 700 warships and thousands of aircraft. General Eisenhower was Commander-in-Chief with Montgomery in charge of the landings. Opposing the Allies the Germans had sixty divisions in northern France and the Low Countries under the command of Field-Marshal Rommel.

Early in April 1944 Allied bombers began to attack railway locomotives, eventually reducing the number of military trains by 80 per cent. They also attacked rail junctions and all kinds of bridges. In the middle of May they switched to airfields and almost wiped out the Luftwaffe in northern France.

THE LANDINGS

D-day—the D stood for Deliverance—was fixed for 5 June but had to be postponed twenty-four hours due to bad weather. Then at 2.00 a.m. on the 6th paratroopers were dropped to guard the flanks of the landing. Seventy-five minutes later 2,000 bombers began to pound the German defences on the beaches, and at 5.50 a.m. they were joined by the guns of Allied warships.

Then at precisely 6.30 a.m. the first waves of troops poured ashore. Alexander Baron described the arrival of one of the later boats:

'The landing craft nosed inshore through a mass of floating rubbish. A dead sailor came floating out to sea, face and legs under water, rump poking upwards; then a dead soldier, his waxen face turned up to the sky, his hands floating palm up-wards on the water; he was kept afloat by his inflated lifebelt. Ahead of them lay beached landing-craft, some wrecked, scattered untidily along the waterline. There was a jarring explosion beneath the bows and the whole craft lurched forward. Men toppled forward in a heap clambered to their feet as the ramps crashed down and ran splashing down into the water. They were all away now and wading with weapons held above their heads towards the wet sand ahead.'

Underwater obstacles, mines, barbed wire and machine-gun posts took heavy toll of the invaders but they came on irresistibly. Within a week they were ten miles inland with 300,000 men safely ashore. Within a month over a million men and 200,000 vehicles had been landed.

The Germans had guessed that invasion was coming but they had expected it at Calais and kept valuable forces there. The troops they had in Normandy were badly positioned, due to arguments between commanders. Although they fought fiercely the Allies soon heavily outnumbered them and had complete control of the air. At Falaise they suffered 250,000 casualties and this led to a general retreat to the Rhine. General Patton's 3rd U.S. Army swept across France and joined forces with the 7th U.S. Army, which had landed on

omigod! what a weapon,

A V2 Rocket ready for launching

the Riviera. The advance forces moved so fast it became very difficult to supply them, particularly with petrol. German resistance at Antwerp lasted until late November and when the port was captured it became the principal target for V-bombs.

BATTLE OF ARNHEM

Montgomery suggested that the Allied armies should 'pack their punch' into the northern sector. Then a lightning drive could be made through the Ruhr, centre of German war industries, to capture Berlin before the Russians. Eisenhower rejected this but gave permission for paratroops to be dropped near the Rhine bridges in Holland. Armoured units would then race up and cross the Rhine. Unfortunately the British airborne units dropped in amongst panzers. After fierce fighting and heavy losses they had to retreat, before the Guards Armoured Division could reach them.

THE BATTLE OF THE BULGE

The Allied armies pressed on towards the Rhine. Hitler and his generals began to call upon the soldiers to fight even more fiercely.

SOLDIERS OF THE ARMY GROUP!
None of us gives up a square foot of German soil while still alive . . . Whoever retreats without giving battle is a traitor to his people . . .
> MODEL,
> Field-Marshal

In desperation Hitler gathered together his last reserves totalling twenty-five divisions and 3,000 tanks. On 15 December 1944, under the cover of heavy fog, he hurled them through the American line in the Ardennes. They were hoping to reach Antwerp but were slowed by fierce American resistance at Bastogne. On being asked to surrender the town General McAuliffe replied—'Nuts!'. Then the fog lifted and thousands of allied planes descended like vultures on the German columns. After a fortnight the advance halted and then the retreat began. The operation had cost Hitler 120,000 men and 600 tanks.

THE RACE TO BERLIN

Meanwhile 300 Russian divisions were swarming across eastern Europe. As in the west the Germans fought with their usual skill and determination but they could not hope to hold back such an enemy. In October the Russians joined forces with Marshal Tito to sweep the Germans out of Yugoslavia and in November began to advance on Budapest. This city was defended fanatically by 150,000 German and Hungarian troops

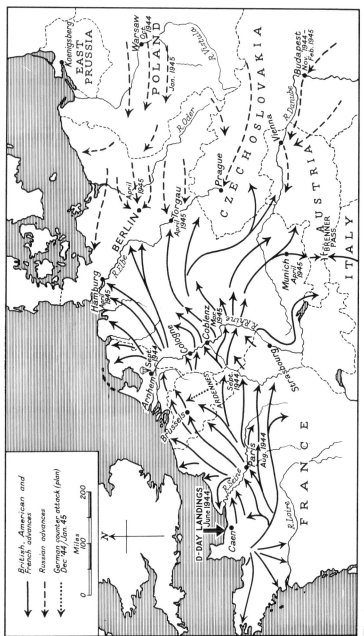

The destruction of Nazi Germany, 1944–45

and was not captured until 13 February 1945. On 12 January 180 Russian divisions attacked through Poland and captured Warsaw. On the 20th Marshal Koniev crossed the German frontier.

In March the British and Americans crossed the Rhine and began to fan out across Germany. On the last day of the month

British Troops advancing into Cleve, 1945

Marshal Zhukov's forces crossed the Oder and prepared to attack Berlin. On 16 April the attack began. On the 18th the last effective German Army in the west was encircled and 300,000 prisoners taken. The British forces raced north to Hamburg and Eisenhower concentrated the Americans to the south and decided to leave Berlin for the Russians. On 25 April the Russians encircled the city and on the same day, at Torgau, units of their 58th Guards Division met up with the U.S. 69th Infantry Division and cut Germany in two.

139

THE END OF NAZI GERMANY

Berlin was defended fiercely by the army, S.S. units and even the Hitler Youth. The Nazis knew the game was up and resolved to sell their lives dearly. Listen to this extract from the diary of a captured officer:

'27th April: Continuous attack throughout the night. Increasing signs of dissolution. . . . Hardly any communication amongst troops, excepting a few regular battalions equipped with radio posts. Telephone cables are shot to pieces. Physical conditions are indescribable. No rest, no relief. No regular food, hardly any bread. We get water from the tunnels and filter it. The whole large expanse of Potsdamer Platz is waste ruins. Masses of damaged vehicles, half-smashed trailers of the ambulances with the wounded still in them. Dead people everywhere, many of them frightfully cut up by tanks and trucks.'

The end could not be long delayed. The German army in Italy had surrendered on 29 April and on 2 May the Berlin garrison followed suit. On 7 May the unconditional surrender was signed at Reims in France. The cease-fire sounded on 8 May 1945, bringing peace to the bloodstained shambles of Europe after nearly six years.

8 MAY 1945[1]

Hasty is the flight of birds. Woe, all that was ever
    ready to soar
Has the weight of stones
That endure under the earth, cemented with the
    bodies and years of love

People have buried their wickedly pampered war
Poppies bloom out of beer.
Paper-chains lace up the bodies of feverish houses.

The wet flags drip into sultry, festive air,
Behind the roll of drums
A skater zigzags over a frozen lake of blood.

[1] Franz Baermann Steiner, 1945. Translated from the German by Michael Hamburger.

THE END OF ADOLF HITLER

Portrait of a warrior. After the attack on Russia in June 1941 Hitler moved to his headquarters known as the Wolf's Lair, at Rastenburg in East Prussia. He remained there until November 1944, when the Russians were overrunning Poland. It was in an isolated spot surrounded by three barbed wire fences and guarded by hundreds of S.S. men. Hitler lived in a bleak concrete bunker and spent most of his time in conference with his generals and in conversation with his cronies. Often these went on far into the night and as usual it was Hitler who did most of the talking. His only exercise was a short daily walk with his Alsatian bitch, Blondi.

As German fortunes in the war declined, Hitler shut himself off more and more from the truth. He lived in the hope of a miracle, either a new weapon or the collapse of the Anglo-American-Russian alliance. He would not visit bombed cities and after Stalingrad made only five broadcasts.

The strain of the war and his unhealthy way of life began to have a serious effect on Hitler's health. Göring said in 1944 that Hitler had aged fifteen years since the war began. The bomb explosion of July 1944 damaged his ears and his nerves, but even more damaging to his health were the drugs he took. To keep himself going under stress Hitler had been 'treated' by Dr Theodore Morell with an enormous variety of narcotics. By the beginning of 1945 Hitler was an addict taking six injections a day. Captain Gerhardt Boldt saw him for the first time in February 1945 and described him thus: 'His head was slightly wobbling. His left arm hung slackly and his hand trembled a good deal. There was an indescribable flickering glow in his eyes, creating a fearsome and wholly unnatural effect.'

General Guderian said: 'He walked awkwardly, stooped more than ever and his gestures were jerky and slow.'

Professor de Giuis believed that Hitler was suffering from Parkinson's disease—a form of paralysis. Dr Geising, another specialist, stated that Morell's drugs were slowly poisoning Hitler, causing stomach cramps and discoloration of the skin.

Hitler goes underground. In mid-January 1945 Hitler returned to the Chancellery building in Berlin. Frequent air raids forced him into his bunker, an enormously strong shelter 50 feet

The last picture of Adolf Hitler. He is congratulating a member of the Hitler Youth who was helping to defend Berlin *Hello little boy! My you have got nice cheeks*

below ground. By the end of March he went into the bunker permanently and never left it again alive. He had planned to leave for Bavaria on his birthday, but the military situation changed his mind and on 22 April he resolved to die in Berlin.

Life in the bunker was the same dreary round as in the Wolf's Lair. Military conferences were held in the afternoon and at midnight, but this time they were about armies and regiments which had ceased to exist. Almost to the end Hitler believed that the 12th Army would come to his rescue. That army, or the remains of it, was fighting off the Russians and trying to reach the Americans to surrender to them instead. Hitler now slept only between 8 a.m. and 11 a.m., a faint shadow of the man he had been.

A momentous week. The last days in the bunker saw a flurry of comings and goings. The most notable departure was Hermann Göring who had been told in 1941 that if Hitler was killed or made helpless he should take over as Führer. Göring asked permission by telegram to take over. Hitler replied by ordering the S.S. to arrest him. Five days later news arrived which, said one witness, 'struck a death blow to the entire assembly'.

A BBC broadcast announced that Heinrich Himmler, Chief of Police and S.S. and Minister of the Interior, had been having secret talks with the Swedish Count Folke Bernadotte. In the hope of saving his neck and even remaining in power Himmler had been discussing the surrender to Eisenhower of German forces in the west.

Himmler's treachery, and the fact that the Russians were less than a mile away, forced Hitler to realise that his hour had come. At 2.00 a.m. he married Eva Braun and then dictated his last will and testament.

It was the same old Adolf Hitler. He attacked the Jews and blamed everything upon them, the war, Germany's defeat, even their own massacre. He told the Germans to fight on and accused the generals of failing him. Then he expelled Göring and Himmler from the Nazi Party and stripped them of all offices and honours. Finally he named his successors—Admiral Doenitz to be Führer, Goebbels the Chancellor and Bormann Party Minister.

Later that day, 29 April, Hitler learned that his fellow dictator Mussolini had been shot and his body disfigured and strung up by the heels in Milan. This reinforced his determination that his body should not provide a similar spectacle and he ordered it to be destroyed by burning.

The following afternoon, 30 April 1945, at 3.30 p.m. Hitler shot himself, and his bride took poison. The bodies were carried up into the garden, soaked in petrol and set alight. During the next two hours 200 litres were poured over the bodies until they were reduced to charred, unrecognisable remains.

One week later, the Third Reich ceased to exist.

IS HITLER DEAD?

In April 1965 the West Berlin authorities issued a warrant for the arrest of Adolf Hitler! No, he has not been discovered alive on a misty Baltic island, or on a cattle ranch in the Argentine. The warrant was issued because the twenty-year period allowable for the arrest of Nazi criminals was due to expire on 8 May 1965. It has now been extended until 1969.

Perhaps you may ask, do the West Berliners believe Hitler is still alive? It is, of course, possible that some do, but the vast majority of people throughout the world accept the fact that Hitler is dead.

The doubt over Hitler's death arises because his body *was* unrecognisable when found by the Russians. Two hundred litres of petrol had done a thorough job upon his mortal remains.

Soon after the collapse of Germany, Professor Hugh Trevor-Roper, then an intelligence officer in the British army, was ordered to make a full investigation into Hitler's last days. The results of his findings were published in 1947, in a book, *The Last Days of Hitler*. He proved beyond doubt that Hitler had married Eva Braun in the bunker and then the pair had committed suicide.

Professor Trevor-Roper's evidence is based mainly upon the cross-examination of forty-two leading Nazi Party officials, S.S. men, doctors, army officers and other people who were with Hitler at the end. Their stories were related in various German cities at different times with no chance of collusion. For example, Erich Kempka, Hitler's chauffeur, gave a detailed description of Hitler's suicide, even down to the make and calibre of the gun used.

Kempka was in American custody, and his story was confirmed by Artur Axmann, the Hitler Youth Leader who, until captured, had been at large in the south of Germany. Their evidence was then further confirmed in 1956 by Heinze Linge, Hitler's valet, and an S.S. bodyguard—Harry Mengerhausen, who had been prisoners of the Russians since the end of the war.

Any possibility of a carefully rehearsed story prepared in the last hours in the bunker can be ruled out. For as Professor Trevor-Roper points out, at first they would have agreed exactly on every point as long as the questions were about parts of their rehearsed story. Then, under detailed questioning, they would have begun to differ. What happened was the reverse. The witnesses at first differed on minor details, as witnesses of, say, a car accident tend to differ. Gradually, there appeared a common thread, a basic agreement running through all their stories.

The attitude of the Russians who captured the bunker and the remains of Hitler was strange. At first they refused to pronounce on Hitler's death. Perhaps they were afraid he would be made into a martyr and legendary hero. They would not permit western doctors to compare his skull with numerous X-ray photographs of him which had been obtained. Then in 1950 a new Russian film called *The Fall of Berlin* was released. It showed Hitler, not escaping, but committing suicide by poison.

In the face of all the evidence to the contrary, it is impossible to believe that a semi-paralysed, ageing drug addict could have crawled out across the rubble of Berlin, escaped past hundreds of Russian soldiers, and made for a destination unknown even to himself.

Resistance to Hitler in Germany

'At 12.42 the bomb exploded with a gigantic crash. Most of the roof of the building fell in and all the windows were blown out. Chaos reigned within. The official stenographer, Berger, was killed. Three officers present, including the unlucky Brandt, died subsequently from their injuries. Two others were badly wounded and four more rather more lightly. Hitler had his hair set on fire, his right leg badly burned, his right arm temporarily paralysed and both eardrums damaged. But he was alive.' (20 July 1944)

Hitler's conference room after the bomb explosion. The arrow indicates the spot where the bomb was placed

Thus does one writer[1] describe the greatest, the most disastrous and the final attempt by Germans to bring an end to the rule of Hitler and the Nazi Party. This particular attempt, which cost over 4,000 Germans their lives, received little praise from the Western Powers. One American newspaper compared it to the work of Chicago gangsters. Yet ill-feeling against the Germans persisted after the war for failing to try to overthrow Hitler sooner.

William L. Shirer believes that the resistance movement 'remained from beginning to the end a small and feeble thing'. It failed, says Gerhard Ritter, 'because no political power came to its aid'. More recent research such as that of Mr Prittie seems to confirm the view of Hans Rothfels that it was 'much more widespread than could have been expected under conditions of terror'. Thus in spite of its failure to overthrow Hitler 'its memory', says Hugh Trevor-Roper, 'has triumphed over the memory of Nazism'.

The resisters came from every branch of German society but they were never united in organisation—only in their hatred of

[1] Terence Prittie, *Germans against Hitler*.

German resistance leader, Carl Goerdeler

Nazism. If the resisters can be said to have had any real leaders the honours must go to General Ludwig Beck and Dr Carl Goerdeler, former Lord Mayor of Leipzig. Beck turned against Hitler because he believed he was leading Germany to disaster and because his conscience was troubled by the brutality of the Nazis. Goerdeler worked and co-operated with the Nazis from 1933 to 1936 but slowly came to understand the evil of their aims and ideas. From early 1937 to his death, he became an unrelenting and energetic enemy of Hitler and the Nazis. He was always on the move encouraging individuals, organising groups and drawing up plans for the future Germany— had the bomb plot of 20 July succeeded, Goerdeler would have succeeded Hitler as Chancellor.

THE CHURCHES

Neither the Catholic nor the Protestant Church resisted the Nazis as organised bodies. However, great numbers of clergy and laymen spoke out and wrote against the Nazis. Bishop von Galen of Muenster made the fiercest attack on the Nazis in 1941, but warned his people: 'It may happen that obedience to God, and loyalty to conscience, can cost you or me life, freedom or home. But it is better to die than to sin.'

Obedience to God's law—'love thy neighbour'—cost Father Bernhard Lichtenberg his life in 1943. Arrested for treason in 1941, it was found that he had been offering up prayers for the Jews for over three years in his church. He died of 'natural causes' on the way to Dachau concentration camp.

Pastor Paul Schneider took twenty months to die at the hands of the S.S. A powerfully built man aged thirty-seven when the Nazis came to power, Schneider spoke his mind freely. He attacked the Hitler Youth Movement, collected money for the Jews, refused to vote in the 1936 elections and called Hitler an agent of the devil. His arrest took place in November 1937; his death on 18 July 1939, finally as a result of a poisonous injection.

'His body was a single festering mass of cuts, scars and bruises. The bones of his legs and other joints were swollen to elephantine proportions by starvation and his wrists (he had been hanged by the arms from his cell window) were coloured blue, green and red in huge blotches.'

The youth of Germany were probably the most fanatical of Hitler's followers. Millions joined the Hitler Youth and millions of young Germans were to die in World War II. But not all young Germans believed in Nazism and many were prepared to die rather than submit to Hitler.

Seventeen-year-old Jonathan Stark, a Jehovah's Witness, refused to join the Army and spoke fearlessly about the evils of Nazism. He was hanged in 1944. Helmut Huebener listened to the BBC and secretly printed leaflets telling the truth about Nazis' practices. In one year he printed twenty different leaflets, distributing hundreds of copies throughout Hamburg. At the age of $17\frac{1}{2}$ he was guillotined.

Perhaps the most spectacular resistance was that of the 'White Rose' Group, centred around Munich University. The leaders were brother and sister Hans and Sophie Scholl who were students, and a professor, Kurt Huber.

Their resistance took the form of 'White Rose' leaflets attacking the slaughter of Jews, Poles and Russians and calling upon the German people to sabotage the war effort. Later ones dealt with the future Germany when freedom and justice would return. Then suddenly in February 1943 the group came to a tragic end.

After listening to a particularly disgusting speech by the local Nazi Party chief, the Scholls decided to make a public act of defiance. They had hundreds of leaflets quickly printed then marched around the University dropping them everywhere. Finally they climbed to the top of the main building and scattered the leaflets over the square and entrance hall.

Within half an hour they were in Gestapo custody and on 19 February, following a 'trial' in the People's Court, they were beheaded. Other members of the group soon met a similar fate.

SOCIALISTS AND COMMUNISTS

It will be remembered that at the last election in March 1933 the Socialists had gained 7 million votes and the Communists nearly 5 million compared to the Nazis 17 million. Why did the two left-wing Parties not join up against the Nazis and try to break their power? Unfortunately the Social

Democrats and the Communists hated each other more than they hated the Nazis. The Communists had orders from Moscow to help the Nazis against the Social Democrats. The Social Democrats themselves were tired out by their efforts to support the Weimar Republic and lacked confidence in themselves to try to overthrow the Nazis. However, they were probably the first to realise the evils of Nazism for they alone voted against the 'Enabling Law'. Many who escaped the first waves of arrests fled to Czechoslovakia, Switzerland, Belgium and France. In these countries they printed newspapers and reports compiled from information smuggled out of Germany.

Willy Brandt, now Mayor of West Berlin, fled to Norway but worked in Spain, Finland, Czechoslovakia, Holland and Berlin itself, where he organised resistance 'cells'. Brandt survived but Carl von Ossietzky, editor of the outspoken *Weltbuchne*, died of ill-treatment in prison. Ossietzky refused either to leave Germany or to be silent about the Nazis. They became keen to release him after he won the 1935 Nobel Peace Prize but his unshakeable courage cost him his life.

Slowly the Social Democrat Party began to establish a network of cells throughout Germany which kept the 'spirit of resistance' alive. The Gestapo hunted down the members of these groups ruthlessly. Some committed suicide to safeguard their secrets; some, like Julius Leber who knew all about the bomb plot of 20 July 1944, resisted agonising tortures and saved their fellow-plotters.

The Communist Party provided some of the toughest anti-Nazi fighters. But like so many others they did not believe, in 1933, that Hitler would last long in power. Nevertheless they began to organise an underground resistance, which resulted in mass arrests and trials. During the period 1939–41 their activities were 'frozen' by the Russo-German Pact (see page 96).

The most successful group was known as the 'Rote Kapelle' (Red Orchestra) led by a dedicated Communist, Harro Schulze-Boysen. Its main purposes were to supply military secrets to Russia and to disrupt the production of German weapons and ammunition. Its members also produced newspapers and stuck posters on the walls under the cover of darkness.

The 'Rote Kapelle' was betrayed in 1942 and a hundred of its members executed. Schulze-Boysen himself 'died like a man' in the Gestapo torture chambers in Berlin. After this Communist resistance was much less effective though no less fierce.

THE KREISAU CIRCLE

We can now see that Hitler and the Nazis were thoroughly hated by large sections of the German people. They all hoped that Nazism would be destroyed and replaced by a new government and a different way of life. The Catholics, the Conservatives and the Communists all had different ideas about what should come after Nazism. But it was a group of forty men, representing nearly every section of German life, who built up the most acceptable and long-lasting plans for the future Germany.

This group met at Kreisau in Silesia, the home of Count Helmuth James von Moltke. The other leader of the Group was Count Peter Yorck von Wartenburg and members of the group included religious, political and educational leaders, civil servants, landowners and former trade unionists. Although they were nearly all executed by the Nazis their ideas—in the words of William L. Shirer, 'sort of a Christian socialism in which all men would be brothers'—have survived. Their plans for a United States of Europe and a united Trade Union movement have been well received in postwar West Germany.

THE ARMY

Father Lichtenberg offered prayers, Pastor Schneider collected money, the Scholls printed leaflets. Major-General Oster warned the Dutch of the coming German invasion in 1940 and Schulze Boysen sent military information to the Russians. The ordinary people of Berlin sheltered 5,000 Jews throughout the war. All admirable and highly dangerous activities; but none of these people could remove the Nazis from power. An uprising would have been mercilessly crushed by the machine-guns, flame-throwers and tanks of the S.S., just as in the Warsaw Ghetto in 1943.

To resist Nazism was one thing, to remove the Nazis from power was beyond the capacity of all Germany—except the army. Only the army had the strength to break the power of the S.S. and Gestapo. Unfortunately, as we have seen, Hitler had begun to secure an iron grip on the army as early as 1934 when every soldier had sworn an oath of loyalty to him. It was also very difficult to expect an army revolt to succeed against a leader who was so successful (up to 1943). Nevertheless there existed a small group of officers, led by General Beck, who made repeated but unsuccessful attempts to topple Hitler from power.

The first serious attempt took place in the autumn of 1938 when it was thought that Hitler was going to order an invasion of Czechoslovakia. Troops in Berlin were to arrest Hitler and those in central Germany were to hold off the S.S. Unfortunately Hitler persuaded Britain and France to grant his requests regarding Czechoslovakia so the attempt never took place.

Further plans came to nothing mainly due to the unwillingness of certain generals to help. Once the war had begun and the German army was going from victory to victory, it became very difficult for the plotters to persuade other officers that Hitler should be removed.

In 1941 a plan to arrest Hitler whilst he was visiting the Russian front proved a failure. The size of his S.S. bodyguard and the precautions taken were too great to be overcome. It was at last realised that the only way to remove Hitler was to kill him outright. In February 1943 the first near-miss occurred. A young officer, Fabian von Schlabrendorff, smuggled a bomb disguised as two brandy bottles onto Hitler's plane. The bomb failed to go off. With incredible courage Schlabrendorff recovered the bottles and dismantled them in the toilet of a night express to Berlin!

During the next ten months at least six attempts were made on Hitler's life—each miraculous escape confirming his belief in his 'divine mission'.

Finally on 20 July 1944 Lt.-Col. Klause Philip Schenk, Count von Stauffenberg, placed his briefcase containing a bomb under the Führer's map table in his headquarters at Rastenburg. Army revolts were planned in Paris, Berlin, Prague and Vienna upon the news of the explosion. As we have seen the bomb did not kill Hitler and his vengeance was terrible.

The German resistance movement shed much blood in perhaps a little reparation for the blood shed by Hitler.

Why Germany Lost the War

Whatever the makers of war films may try to tell us, Germany was primarily defeated because after 1942 she was heavily outnumbered in men, tanks, guns and aeroplanes. The combined populations and production of the British Commonwealth, the U.S.A. and the U.S.S.R. far exceeded that of Germany and her allies. Of Germany's two main allies Italy had no heart to fight, while Japan gave her no help at all.

HITLER'S MISTAKES

Before Germany became outnumbered, Hitler had an excellent chance of winning the war. His first mistake was in not having carefully planned an invasion of Britain. If Britain had been conquered the U.S.A. would have had no base in Europe from which to attack Germany. In fact it is highly doubtful if the U.S.A. would have made any attempt to defeat Germany single-handed. Many people believe Hitler's greatest mistake was attacking the U.S.S.R. When we remember how close he came to capturing Leningrad, Moscow and Stalingrad, we can see that his main mistake had lain in his handling of the campaign. The postponement of the attack on Russia to fight in the Balkans resulted in the Wehrmacht being caught by the terrible winter when still short of their targets. In 1942 the campaign led to the disaster at Stalingrad when Hitler should have been aiming at Moscow to destroy Russian railway communications.

Failing to realise the importance of North Africa, Hitler neglected it until defeat was inevitable. Lack of German seapower gave the Allies an enormous advantage which Hitler also underrated. By September 1944 Hitler had still got 10 million men under arms but they were scattered all over Europe. Instead of bringing them back to the German frontiers he was still using the tactics of 'Stand fast and fight' which had brought disaster at Stalingrad. Hitler's trouble was that he rarely learnt by experience. Having won in France and

Poland by attacking, he tried to turn the tide in 1943 and 1944 by attacks when he should have been shortening his fronts for defence. When his ideas had succeeded against the advice of his generals, Hitler believed he would never fail; will-power and determination would be enough.

TOTAL WAR

Not until it was too late did Germany try to fight a 'total' war —that is using all her population and resources to the full. In October 1941 believing Russia to be finished Hitler ordered the army to start disbanding certain divisions! Britain mobilised women into the armed services and factories. Hitler was against this idea, and as a result men were kept out of the armed forces to do jobs which women could well have done. Even at the height of the war there were over a million female domestic servants who could presumably have worked in ammunition factories.

To some extent slave workers (see page 154) helped Germany's war effort but they did as little as possible and some sabotaged weapons and equipment.

'Total' war means the concentration of all industries, materials and manpower upon the war effort. As an example, look through some lists of used cars for sale. You will not find a British make dated between 1940 and 1945. The car factories were turning out vehicles for the armed forces.

Nazi Germany never had this concentration of effort, only of plans. Professor Trevor-Roper called it a 'confusion of private empires, private armies and private intelligence services'. Even with defeat staring them in the face, top Nazis like Bormann were more concerned with their own ambitions than winning the war.

The German soldier was a highly trained, brave and disciplined man. He brought Nazism to within an ace of conquering Europe. But the victory was elusive and when the full weight of Allied power was brought to bear Nazi Germany was pounded to ruins.

Europe under the Swastika

For millions of Europeans the German occupation of their homelands was one long nightmare. In general treatment varied according to race. Thus the 'Aryan' Danes and Nor-wegians were regarded favourably and the French, Belgians and Dutch rather less so. The unfortunate inhabitants of Russia, Poland and Yugoslavia were, in the eyes of the Nazis, sub-humans and fit only to be their slaves. For the Jews there was to be one fate only—death.

PLUNDER

The Nazis fought to make Germany richer and stronger. Occupied territories were forced to pay various taxes which according to one American survey came to a grand total of £6,000 million. In addition vast quantities of food, livestock and raw materials were seized without payment. In 1943 nearly 15 million tons of food were taken from Russia; during the whole war over 30 million cattle, sheep and pigs were taken. All this meant that the inhabitants of the plundered countries were extremely short of food themselves.

SLAVE LABOUR

As the war progressed Germany became increasingly short of manpower. As men were taken from factories to replace casualties at the front it occurred to the Nazi leaders that the conquered lands could provide the workers. Russian prisoners-of-war, inmates of concentration camps and civilians of all countries were used. S.S. units surrounded villages and carried off all able-bodied men and women; in the same way the Press Gang had operated in eighteenth-century England. At least 5 million slaves were working in Germany by late 1944, a tiny fraction compared with what would have occurred if the Nazis had won the war. Dr Wilhelm Jaiger told the court at Nuremberg of a visit to a slave camp.

'Upon my first visit I found these females suffering from open festering wounds and other diseases. I was the first doctor they had seen for a fortnight. . . . There were no medical supplies. . . . They had no shoes. The sole clothing of each consisted of a sack with holes for their arms and head. Their hair was shorn. The amount of food in the camp was extremely meagre and of very poor quality. One could not enter the barracks without being attacked by fleas. . . . I got large boils on my arms and the rest of my body from them. . . .'

PRISONERS-OF-WAR

Under the Hague and Geneva Conventions soldiers were given protection when they were captured. Russia had not signed these conventions but even if she had it is doubtful if it would have saved her captured soldiers. Five million Russian soldiers were captured by the Germans; 2 million died in captivity and another million cannot be accounted for. During the first terrible winter 1941–42 enormous numbers were left out in the open to die of cold and hunger. The Nazis felt they had no obligation to feed the captured Russians with the result, said Göring laughingly, that '. . . after having eaten everything possible including the soles of their boots they have begun to eat each other and what is more serious, have eaten a German sentry'.

Understandably the Russians replied in a similar manner. A German soldier told how his section had seen a block of ice outside a Russian village with ten German helmets on top. When they came close they were horrified to find the ice encased the bodies of ten Germans roped together. They had been captured by partisans, who had stripped them of their clothing and thrown buckets of water over them until they became frozen solid.

Later prisoners were used as slaves in factories, on anti-aircraft guns and for clearing minefields.

British and American P.O.W.s were treated much better than the Russians. There were some noticeable incidents of barbarism such as the massacre of fifty airmen after the 'Great Escape'. Commando troops who specialised in raids behind the German lines were, on Hitler's orders, to be shot immediately upon capture.

These murders were carried out almost entirely by the S.S. and Gestapo. On more than one occasion Wehrmacht and Luftwaffe officers held on to Allied prisoners against orders in an effort to prevent them falling into the hands of Hitler's butchers.

TERROR

In every German-occupied territory a resistance movement sprang up. Attacks were made by partisans upon German stores, barracks, trains, convoys and troops. The killing of

Captured Polish resistance men. The German officer is inspecting their home-made weapons

German soldiers brought terrible reprisals upon the population, usually by shooting hostages. In Denmark five were killed for every German, in Yugoslavia the number was 300.

Another method of striking terror into the hearts of the conquered was Hitler's Night and Fog Decree. By this order anyone regarded as an enemy was kidnapped and disappeared without a trace into the night and fog. Relatives were not told one word of the victim's fate.

These victims, in the company of many resistance men and Jews, were brought to concentration camps. Driven on by indescribable torture and brutality these unfortunates were to be 'worked to death' in great factories built alongside the camps. Many were owned by the S.S. Many inmates survived these camps but scarcely one emerged alive from the extermination camps.

THE FINAL SOLUTION

Before the war began Hitler harried and hounded the Jews of Germany. Thousands took refuge abroad, thousands were imprisoned, a 'few' were killed and some found refuge with non-Jewish friends. Germany had half a million Jews but in the rest of Europe there were about 11 million. In the course of long and secret talks with Himmler, Hitler conceived the most horrific plan of all time. Every Jewish man, woman and child in Europe was to be transported to eastern Europe and exterminated. This was Hitler's 'final solution' to the Jewish problem.

At one time Hitler had toyed with the idea of transporting all the Jews to the island of Madagascar but this was eventually rejected as impossible. When Poland was invaded all Jews were driven into ghettoes, sections of large cities which were walled off. Rations were reduced to starvation level but this method was proving too slow. Camps were therefore established to liquidate the Jews at Belzek, Treblinka, Maideneck and Auschwitz-Birkenau.

Eventually from all over Europe Jews were transported to the death-factories, of which Auschwitz has become most notorious. Upon arrival they marched past two S.S. doctors who sent them either to the factories to be worked to death or straight to the gas chambers. At his trial the Commandant Rudolf Höss described the operation after the unsuspecting victims had been crowded into the gas chambers disguised as showers.

'At Auschwitz I used Zyklon B, which was a crystallised prussic acid which we dropped into the death chamber from a small opening. It took from three to fifteen minutes to kill all the people in the death chamber. We knew when the people were dead because their screaming stopped.'

Six thousand people a day could be gassed at Auschwitz. In all about one million passed through its gates during its three years of operation. Another three-quarters of a million died at the hands of the '*Einsatzgruppen*'—special action squads —in Russia. The victims here were made to dig their own graves and were then shot in the back.

By the end of the war Hitler had destroyed over one-third of Europe's Jews. About $4\frac{1}{2}$ million human beings, of whom 900,000 were under fourteen years old, paid the price of one man's twisted hatred.

5 Hitler's Legacy: 1945—?

The Cost of the War

The number of dead will never be known exactly. Several estimates have been made and mostly they fall in the region of 30 to 40 million. This includes those killed in the war against Japan in the Far East. Hitler's war must have cost at least 25 million lives. The material damage is likewise impossible to estimate but we can get some idea from the damage done to Russia which suffered most. After the war the Soviet Government listed the following completely destroyed:

1,700 towns and 70,000 villages
5 million houses
82,000 schools and colleges
98,000 collective farms
71 million farm animals.

They estimated the total damage at £30,000 million and the death roll at over 12 million.

France and Britain suffered much less than Russia but both had about half a million houses destroyed. The road and rail communications of France were battered into ruins and in 1945 her agricultural production was down 50 per cent on 1939. Britain lost about 5,000 ships ranging from battleships to motor-boats, and after paying £16 million per day on the war effort was near to bankruptcy by 1945.

The fierce resistance of Marshal Tito's partisans and the subsequent retaliation of the Germans ended in the death of one out of every nine adults in Yugoslavia. Poland lost over 6 million dead, and the capital Warsaw was systematically destroyed building by building after the unsuccessful uprising of August 1944.

In Germany every great city was a rubble heap. Seventy-five per cent of Cologne lay in ruins while 'Berlin', wrote a Russian reporter, 'is a city of desolation and shattered dreams inhabited by a half-mad, half-starving population, clawing its frenzied way into battered food shops, slinking for shelter into cellars and currying favour with the conqueror'.

Two and a half million German civilians perished in the ruins of these cities and in refugee columns from the east. Three million German soldiers fell on the battlefields of Russia, France, Italy and North Africa. Another million were marched off to the dreary prison camps of Siberia from which few were ever to emerge alive.

According to the official calculation of the West German Government in 1959 a total of 7,032,800 Germans perished in Hitler's war.

Paying the Price

As soon as the war ended an enormous man-hunt began in Europe for the major war criminals. Many, like Adolf Eichmann, escaped either by changing their identities or by going abroad. Spain and South America seem to have been the favourite destinations.

Eventually about 22,000 stood trial of whom 1,500 were sentenced to death and 15,000 imprisoned. The remainder were acquitted. World attention was chiefly centred upon the trial of the major war criminals at Nuremberg. Twenty-one of them sat in the dock, headed by Hermann Göring. They were accused of waging aggressive war and of crimes against humanity. Hundreds of witnesses and sworn statements were heard; the accused were given the best lawyers possible and allowed to speak for as long as they wished. Göring was in the witness box for three days.

At long last the verdicts were reached. Three were acquitted, seven received prison sentences ranging from ten years to life and the remaining eleven were sentenced to be hanged. The sentences were carried out on the morning of 16 October 1946, only Hermann Göring managing to cheat the gallows by taking poison.

The Changed Face of Europe

Britain went to war with Germany in 1939 to prevent her gaining control of most of Europe. While taking part in the destruction of German military power Britain allowed another nation, Russia, to overshadow Europe. Nazism was conquered but Communism increased enormously in power. Communist 'puppet' governments were set up in all the eastern European countries overrun by the Russians.

Germany was divided into two sections—the largest in the West under British, American and French control, the East under the Russians. Berlin, deep within the Russian Zone, was also divided amongst the four powers. The wartime co-operation of Russia and the Western Allies soon dissolved and an 'iron curtain' descended across Europe.

Hitler set out to conquer and unite Europe. He ended by dividing it completely.

The Guilt of the German People

Adolf Hitler must be a leading candidate for the title of the 'most evil man who ever lived'. Although he was the complete master of Germany and, for a time, most of Europe, he needed a great deal of willing help to carry out his monstrous plans. From thousands of S.S. and Gestapo, Nazi Party officials and some great industrialists, he received such help. In addition, he undoubtedly received the moral support of many of those whose votes had put him into power.

The enormous cost and slaughter of World War II, and the sickening revelations from Auschwitz and similar places, created intense bitterness, often amounting to open hatred, towards the whole German nation. A popular saying during and after the war was 'the only good German is a dead one'. Such feelings are understandable in those who suffered or witnessed the worst horrors of Nazism. Whilst it is impossible to find any excuse for Hitler and his Nazi murder squads, does the whole German nation, collectively and individually, bear the guilt for the atrocities of the Third Reich?

Hitler could not have carried out his plans if he (and the Nazis) had not got into power. If we recall the events of 1932–33, we will remember that the Nazis were not voted into office. In the last free and fair election in November 1932 the Nazi poll came to only 37 per cent. Nearly two-thirds of the German electorate rejected Hitler. He came into power through back-stairs consultations and shady deals. We should also remember that 1932 was hardly a normal year. The unemployment figure was over 5 million, and the Weimar Republic seemed to have failed completely. Hitler was the only genuine alternative for those who had lost confidence in the Republic. It can be argued that Hitler was offering such an evil programme that no decent person should have voted for him. The question then arises—how many Germans, in spite of the posters, rallies and marches, really understood the Nazi programme? During the 1964 British General Election, a television survey found that well over half the people who had watched a party political broadcast the previous night had little or no idea of what it was all about!

Still, those who voted for Hitler in 1933 cannot be completely blameless. A great many *did* know what Nazism meant. When we condemn Nazism, however, we usually have the massacre of the Jews in mind, but the mass murders did not get under way until 1941. The decision to exterminate the Jews was the fruit of long, highly secret discussions between Heydrich, Himmler and Hitler himself in 1940. Although Hitler made the lives of German Jews progressively more unbearable after 1933, he did not deliberately kill them, though many died from ill-treatment. It is scarcely credible that any

Great match! I think Everton will win

Prisoners at Auschwitz

German who voted Nazi in 1932 could have guessed that Hitler would murder 4½ million Jews. Once the massacres did start it was difficult to keep them secret from the civilian population. Too many packed trains returned empty; too much black stinking smoke passed out of the camp crematoria chimneys, too many staggering emaciated figures were seen working outside the camps, driven on by the kicks and blows of the S.S. guards.

Granted, then, that a large number of Germans were fully aware of the massacre of the Jews, what could they have done about it? In a magazine article, the distinguished historian, A. J. P. Taylor, suggested that they might have derailed trains carrying Jews to their death, or shot some S.S. men in the back. These methods were often employed by Frenchmen, Poles, Russians and Yugoslavs against their German conquerors. The result was usually a holocaust of revenge against innocent people. The assassination of former Gestapo Chief Heydrich in 1942 cost the lives of 5,000 Czechs. There is little reason to suppose that Hitler would have shown greater mercy to, say, the villagers of Bergen-Belsen for a similar action. The Germans had had six years longer than the rest of Europe to learn what resistance to Hitler meant.

It is, of course, very easy to suggest the others should have been selfless and prepared to sacrifice their lives for 'freedom' and 'justice'. Sooner or later each of you will have the chance to stand up to a bully or a thug. At the worst you are likely to get a good hiding. Will you stand your ground, or will you beat a quick and silent retreat? This was the choice facing millions of Germans in Hitler's time. They faced not only a beating, but the possibility of a slow and agonising death. Hitler did not hesitate to take revenge against the families of his enemies either.

What of the war? At least 10 million young Germans fought in the armies which laid waste Europe—what guilt do they bear?

Most observers agree that the events of 1939 did not bring out cheering crowds into the streets of German towns. A general air of gloom hung over Berlin on 1 September when Hitler drove to the Kroll Opera House to address the Reichstag (Parliament). This was a marked contrast to the frenzied crowds who filled the main squares of Europe's capitals in August 1914. Nevertheless, a great many German soldiers and civilians were obviously filled with pride by the early victories (1939–42). But one has only to watch British and American films to realise that this type of national pride is not confined to Germany. You may argue that Germany was waging an evil, aggressive war upon helpless and innocent countries. Therefore, in spite of the fact that Nazi propaganda tried hard to justify the war, should not the army have refused to obey orders and even tried to overthrow Hitler? This argument brings us on to dangerous ground. The British, with the world's largest Empire (in 1939), are amongst the last people in the world to accuse foreigners of seizing other people's territories. A German could point to the British conquest of the Boers, the French in West Africa, the Russians in eastern Asia, or the near extinction of the Amerindians, and ask when exactly is a war just? None of the above-mentioned conquests can remotely compare with the eventual evils of Nazism, but once again we must remember that the German armies overrunning Western Europe in 1940 could not know that Auschwitz would be opened eighteen months later. By the time most German soldiers did realise what was happening to the Jews, Germany was locked in a life and death battle with the Allied Powers. The ordinary soldier, whose role, Kipling tells us, is 'not to reason why', would by then have had his hands full just fighting and staying alive. Even the men who tried to kill Hitler in 1944 spent hours wrestling with their consciences about the morality of their plans at a time when Germany was in mortal danger.

Many German soldiers committed acts of great savagery against the civilian population and prisoners-of-war, particularly Russians. These acts were totally inexcusable. Much of the guilt for these must also rest with Hitler. Before the attack on Russia Hitler promised that no German would be punished for an offence against a Russian, and fear of punishment is surely the greatest deterrent to wrong-doing. Nazism is probably the worst experience (so far) which mankind has been through. It is certainly not the only example of 'man's inhumanity to man' in recent years. According to one American estimate in 1950 there were nearly 20 million slave labourers in Soviet Russia, of whom the majority died in captivity. The Americans themselves were guilty of many atrocities against the native Indian population during the opening of the West. The Belgian seizure of the Congo in the late nineteenth century cost several hundred thousand lives as a result of the brutal rule of King Leopold's agents. During the years immediately before World War I, nearly a million Armenians died at the hands of their Turkish rulers. The death roll in the Spanish Civil War (1936–39) reached the half million mark, and about the same number of Indians died at each other's hands following Independence in 1947.

None of these terrible wrongs makes Nazism right. Indeed, it can be argued that since some of the above horrors were committed in war, in 'hot blood', they make the cold-blooded deliberate extermination policies of Hitler seem even more ghastly. But they also show us that inhumanity is far from being confined solely within the frontiers of Germany.

In Conclusion

'National Socialism', wrote Alan Bullock, 'produced nothing. The sole theme of the Nazi revolution was domination dressed up as the doctrine of race and failing that a vindictive destructiveness. It is this emptiness, this lack of anything to justify the suffering he caused . . . which makes Hitler so repellent and so barren a figure.'

Biographical Notes

BLOMBERG, Field-Marshal W. von (1878–1943)
Minister of Defence 1932. Minister of War 1935. Supported Hitler in Röhm purge, but disagreed with Blitzkrieg methods. Resigned all offices in 1938.

BORMANN, Martin (1900–45)
Joined Nazis 1920, secretary to Hess 1931. Chief of Nazi Party 1941. Hated Christianity. Believed killed in Berlin trying to escape through Russian lines.

BRÜNING, Heinrich (1885–   )
Centre Party Deputy 1924. Chancellor 1930–32 during Great Depression. Left Germany 1933.

DARRE, Walther (1895–1953)
Joined Nazis 1930. Minister of Agriculture 1933. Dismissed by Hitler 1943.

EICHMANN, Adolf (1906–62)
Head of Anti-Jewish Office of Gestapo. Supervised execution of 400,000 Hungarian Jews 1944. Kidnapped by Israeli agents in Argentine 1960. Long trial in Jerusalem. Executed.

FRANK, Hans (1900–46)
Lawyer. Minister of Justice in Bavaria. Governor-General of Poland 1939–44. Executed at Nuremberg.

FRICK, Wilhelm (1877–1945)
Policeman. Nazi Deputy 1924. Minister of Interior 1933. Reponsible for laws against Jews 1935. Dismissed 1943. Executed at Nuremberg 1946.

GOEBBELS, Paul Joseph (1897–1945)
Doctor of Philosophy. Author and playwright. Party boss in Berlin. Minister of Propaganda 1933. Committed suicide 1945. Crippled, brilliant speaker, highly intelligent, completely loyal to Hitler.

GÖRING, Reichsmarshal Hermann (1893–1946)
Minister of Luftwaffe 1933. In charge of German economy 1937–42. Committed suicide in death cell at Nuremberg. Luxury-loving, wore garish uniforms. Took drugs, plundered art galleries of Europe, head game-warden of Reich.

HESS, Rudolf (1894–   )
Deputy Führer 1933. Flew to Scotland 1941 in vain hope of arranging peace. Life sentence at Nuremberg. Still in Spandau Prison, Berlin (1967).

HIMMLER, Heinrich (1900–45)
Head of S.S. 1929 and all German police 1936. Minister of Interior 1943. Commander of Home Army 1944. In overall charge of Jewish massacres and other horrors. Deserted Hitler at the end. Committed suicide when captured by British troops.

KEITEL, Field-Marshal Wilhelm (1882–1946)
Head of Military High Command 1938. Worked closely with Hitler in planning war. Signed surrender of German forces 1945. Executed at Nuremberg.

LEY, Robert (1890–1946)
Early Nazi Party member. Party boss in Cologne until 1932. Leader of Labour Front 1933 after destruction of Trade Unions. Threatened strikers with executions. Organised slave labour. Committed suicide at Nuremberg.

PAPEN, Franz von (1879–   )
Served in German Embassies in Mexico and Washington (1915). Chancellor 1932. Helped Hitler become Chancellor. Ambassador in Vienna (1936–38). Acquitted at Nuremberg.

RIBBENTROP, Joachim von (1893–1946)
Champagne salesman. Joined Nazis 1932. Foreign Minister 1938–45 after serving as Ambassador to Britain. Executed at Nuremberg.

SCHACHT, Hjalmar (1877–   )
Banker and politician. Supported Hitler after 1930. Minister of Economics 1934–37. Imprisoned by Nazis 1944. Acquitted of war crimes 1946. Returned to banking 1953.

SCHLEICHER, General Kurt von (1882–1934)
Served in Ministry of Defence, dabbling in politics. Minister of Defence 1932. Chancellor 1932. Killed by S.S. on 30 June 1934.

SPEER, Albert (1905–   )
Architect and politician. Worked on planning of Autobahn. Minister of Munitions and Armaments 1942. Designed Atlantic Wall. Sentenced to twenty years at Nuremberg for using slave labour. Released 1966.

Glossary

Political Terms

COMMUNISM

The system under which all citizens share a common owner-
ship of all property. This means all factories, shops, banks,
transport, etc., are nationalised. Communism also teaches that
all citizens should share equally in the wealth of the country.
Individual freedom is subordinated to party rule.

The idea of Communism was first developed by Karl Marx
and Friedrich Engels in their *Communist Manifesto* published in
1847. Until 1918 the followers of Marx were usually called
Socialists or Social Democrats. In 1918 Lenin broke away from
accepted socialist movements and founded the Communist
International.

The main difference between Communism and Socialism
(in theory) is that Communism promises a society in which
money and wages will be abolished and everything will be free.
Socialism retains the use of money and the payment of wages.
Russia now claims to be fully socialised (Union of Soviet
Socialist Republics), and to be working towards complete
Communism.

DEMOCRACY

The government of the people, for their common good, by
themselves—that is by their freely elected representatives
(M.P.s, deputies, senators).

How democracy should work. 1. The main theme of a democratic
state is the dignity, freedom and importance of each individual
person. All people are treated as equal especially before the
law, e.g. a poor man accused of a crime will be provided, free
of charge, with a skilled and independent lawyer to defend
him. The individual must be free from arrest without just
cause and from imprisonment without trial.

2 A democracy is a free country. The citizens are free to write,
meet together, make requests, move around, teach and worship

as they wish. Democracies normally allow their citizens to own property and set themselves up in business.

3 Every citizen of a democracy has a right to take part in government. Elections are held frequently and regularly and (with a few exceptions) every adult has the right to vote or stand for election. Voting is secret and anonymous. The elected representatives have the sole authority to make laws and raise taxes. They have complete freedom of speech and freedom from arrest.

4 Decisions are taken on the vote of the majority, but racial and religious minorities should be protected.

5 There should be at least two political parties. Nazi Germany and Soviet Russia, for example, abolished the opposition parties.

6 There should be a complete separation between, and independence of, the legislature (parliament), the executive (government and civil service), and the Judiciary (law courts).

LIBERALISM

A strong belief in individual freedom, democracy and free enterprise.

PACIFISM

The movement for the abolition of war and international disarmament. All disputes to be settled in the International Court of Justice. Eventually it is hoped there would be a World Government.

Political Parties of the Weimar Republic

(*a*) The Moderates who upheld the Republic.

SOCIAL DEMOCRATS

Founded in 1875 mainly through the efforts of Friedrich Lassalle, a middle-class Jew with a reputation for wild and romantic exploits. He died in a duel with a Rumanian nobleman, fought over a girl. Lassalle was anti-Marxist, though the party did contain Marxist ideas. He preferred to work closely with the government. Attacks on socialism by Chancellor

Bismarck led the party into a position of strong opposition to Imperial Germany (1880–1918).

The Social Democrats were the largest party of the Republic until 1932. The Independent Socialists broke away from the main party between 1917 and 1922, reaching their peak year in 1920, when they secured 5 million votes.

CENTRE PARTY

Founded in 1870 by the Roman Catholics in Germany.

Chancellor Bismarck launched an attack on the Catholic Church (*Kulturkampf*) to which the Catholics replied by founding the party. As the common bond of the party was religion and not a political creed, it was able to support various other parties from time to time.

BAVARIAN PEOPLE'S PARTY

The Bavarian Branch of the Centre Party.

DEMOCRATS

Were mainly the remnants of the old Liberal or Progressive Party. Started strongly in 1919 but lost support progressively up to 1933.

GERMAN PEOPLE'S PARTY

Formerly the National Liberal Party, a strong group of businessmen and industrialists who had supported free trade during Bismarck's Chancellorship. They also supported his attacks on the Church and so played some role in government. Under the wise leadership of Gustav Stresemann, they were an active force in the Republic, but declined after his death in 1929.

(*b*) The extreme Right-Wing Parties.

THE NATIONAL SOCIALISTS

Led by Adolf Hitler.

THE NATIONALISTS

The former Conservative Party based on the wealth and power of the great industrialists, landowners and nobility. The

Nationalists were completely and unalterably opposed to the Treaty of Versailles and the Weimar Republic itself. Grew rapidly in strength up to 1924. Overshadowed by the Nazis after 1929.

(*c*) The extreme Left Wing.

THE COMMUNISTS

The Communist Party was the German branch of the Russian Communist Party. Wanted to see Germany follow Russia's example, and gained between 10 and 15 per cent of the votes in the general elections. Stalin, the Russian dictator, ordered them to treat the Social Democrats, not the Nazis, as the major enemy.

In addition, there were many small splinter parties with no real power, devoted to regional or sectional interests, e.g. The Christian National Peasant and Agricultural Popular Party.

Further Reading

The amount of literature available on the history of Nazi Germany and World War II is enormous. Here is a small selection of useful and interesting books. Those of which a paperback edition has been published are marked with an asterisk.

Background Reading

*A. BULLOCK, *Hitler: A Study in Tyranny*. Odhams, 1952; Penguin.

M. GILBERT, *The European Powers 1900–1945*. Weidenfeld and Nicolson, 1965.

K. PINSON, *Modern Germany*. Macmillan of New York, 1954.

*W. L. SHIRER, *The Rise and Fall of the Third Reich*. Secker, 1960; Pan.

Special Topics

*E. CRANKSHAW, *Gestapo—Instrument of Tyranny*. Putnam, 1956; Panther.

R. MANVELL and H. FRAENKEL, *Dr Goebbels*. Heinemann, 1960.

—— *Hermann Göring*. Heinemann, 1962.

—— *Heinrich Himmler*. Heinemann, 1965.

T. PRITTIE, *Germans against Hitler*. Hutchinson, 1964.

*H. TREVOR-ROPER, *The Last Days of Hitler*. 3rd edn. Macmillan, 1956; Pan.

World War II

*P. BAMM, *The Invisible Flag*. Faber, 1956; Penguin.

*K. BURT and J. LEASOR, *The One that Got Away*. Collins, 1956; Fontana.

C. FALLS, *The Second World War*. 3rd edn. Methuen, 1950.

*ANNE FRANK, *The Diary of a Young Girl.* Vallentine, Mitchell, 1952; Pan (as *Anne Frank's Diary*).

A. GALLAND, *The First and the Last.* Methuen, 1955.

A. CLARK, *Barbarossa.* Hutchinson, 1965.

H. SCHAEFFER, *U-Boat 977.* Kimber, 1952.

H. W. SCHMIDT, *With Rommel in the Desert.* Harrap, 1951.

H. SPEIDEL, *We Defended Normandy.* Jenkins, 1951.

*R. WHEATLEY, *Operation Sea Lion.* Oxford University Press, 1958.

*W. ZAGORSKI, *Seventy Days.* Muller, 1958; Panther.

Index

Index

Ebert, Frederick, 22–4
Eckhart, Dietrich, 38
Egypt, 126, 128
Eisenhower, General D. D., 129, 134, 136, 139
Eisner, Kurt, 23
El Alamein, 128, 129
Enabling Law, 61, 77

Fascists (Italian), 32, 41
Faulhaber, Cardinal M., 67
Feder, Gottfried, 34, 35
Final Solution, *see* Jews
Finland, 32
France, 17, 25–31, 40, 48, 82, 99, 108–12
Francis, Joseph, 8, 11
Franco, General F., 86
Frank, Anne, 2, 3, 5
Free Corps, 23–24
Fritsch, General W. von, 73
Fuller, Major-General J., 105

Galen, Cardinal von, 67
George VI, 92
Gestapo, 5, 76, 88, 150, 155
Goebbels, Dr J., 55, 143
Goerdeler, Dr C., 147
Göring, Hermann, 39, 42, 43, 76, 93, 111, 142–3, 159
Graf, Ulrich, 43
Greece, 32, 115
Groener, General, 23
Guderian, General H., 100

Hacha, Dr Emil, 93, 94
Hamburg, 22, 42, 47, 103, 139
Hanisch, Reinhardt, 10
Hanover, 22
Harzburg Front, 55
Henlein, Konrad, 90
Hess, Rudolph, 39, 42
Heydrich, Reinhardt, 76, 161–2
Himmler, Heinrich, 42, 74, 76, 88, 131, 142–3, 157, 161
Hindenburg, Field Marshal P. von, 20, 48, 49, 55, 58
HITLER, ADOLF: Private Life, 10–16, 18–20, 23, 32, 48, 59–60; Nazi Leader, 33–9, 41–5, 49–59; Führer, 61–86; War Lord, 4, 6, 86, 97, 100–43
Hitler Youth, 70, 139

Holland, 20, 30, 108–9, 136
Hugenburg, Alfred, 52
Hungary, 32, 91

Inflation, 39–41, 47
Inter-Allied Commission of Control, 30
Italy, 17, 32, 41, 82, 98, 99, 129–133

Japan, 17, 32, 83, 98, 121, 152, 158
Jews: Former Persecutions of, 13; Hitler's attitude to, 13, 14, 19, 35, 36, 65, 71, 80; Nazi Persecution of, 65, 66, 79; Extermination of, 76, 82, 154, 156, 157, 160–2

Kahr, Gustav von, 42, 43
Kaiser (Wilhelm II), 20
Keitel, Field Marshal von W., 122
Kellogg Pact, 49
Kiev, 118
Kiel, 22
Kleist, Field Marshal von, 110
Koniev, Marshal, 139
Kreisau Circle, 150
Krupps, 30, 70
Kursk, battle of, 125

Landsberg Prison, 45
League of German Maidens, 70
League of Nations, 27, 31, 49, 83, 85, 98, 99
Leeb, Field Marshal von, 118
Lend-Lease, 114
Leningrad, 117, 118, 125
Leopold III of Belgium, 109
Liebknecht, Karl, 23
Lloyd George, 25
Locarno Pact, 49
London, Treaty of, 32
Lossow, General von, 41, 42, 43
Lubbe, M. Van der, 61
Lüdendorff, General E., 20, 21, 43–5
Luftwaffe, 101, 102, 111–14, 128
Luxemburg, Rosa, 23

Maginot Line, 83, 100–1, 108
Manchuria, 98
Manstein, Field Marshal von, 109
Max, Prince, 20, 22
Mein Kampf, 11, 24, 45, 65, 79, 82
Memel, 82, 95
Miklas, President, 87

174

Index

YEAR	WAR IN WESTERN EUROPE	WAR IN EASTERN EUROPE
1939	SEPT British troops land in France	SEPT Germany attacks Poland NOV Russia attacks Finland
1940	APL German invasion of Norway and Denmark MAY German invasion of Western Europe	MAR Russo-Finnish Peace Treaty AUG Russians absorb Baltic States
1941	JULY U.S. forces land in Iceland DEC U.S.A. enters War	JUNE Germany attacks Russia SEPT Leningrad besieged DEC Russian counter-attack at Moscow
1942	AUG Canadian raid on Dieppe NOV Germans occupy Vichy France	JULY Germans capture Sevasto pol SEPT Germans attack Stalingra NOV Russian counter-attack a Stalingrad
1943	JAN Allies demand unconditional surrender	FEB Germans surrender at Stalingrad JULY Russian victory at Kursk
1944	JUNE D-Day landings SEPT Belgium liberated DEC German counter-attack	JAN Leningrad freed after $2\frac{1}{2}$ years siege JULY Russians enter Poland NOV Budapest encircled
1945	MAR Allies cross Rhine APL Americans and Russians meet at Torgau	JAN Russians capture Warsav MAY 8TH Surrender of all Germa